LET'S

EAT

Spanish

LET'S EAT

Spanish

Therese Avila-Lupé

**Editor
Wendy Hobson**

foulsham

LONDON • NEW YORK • TORONTO • SYDNEY

foulsham

Yeovil Road, Slough, Berkshire, SL1 4JH

ISBN 0-572-01835-5

Photoset in Great Britain by Encounter Photosetting, Fleet, Hampshire
Printed in Great Britain by Cox & Wyman Ltd, Reading, Berkshire

Contents

Introduction

Until relatively recently, the cuisine of Spain had not travelled far beyond the borders of that fascinating country. Many visitors to Spain experienced the international cuisine offered in so many hotels and restaurants which, though it may have had Spanish overtones, gave no real clue to the scope and delights of the real Spanish cookery which was taking place in the home.

Because Spain is such a large country, the different regions have developed their own distinctive culinary features. This is hardly surprising since the climate varies from the mild north to the hot and sultry south, with rugged mountains and fertile valleys between. The seasons play their part, too, bringing different foods into play to extend the variety and range of the dishes prepared. Nourishing game stews from the mountains contrast wonderfully with delectable seafood dishes from the coastal regions or grilled meats and vegetables from the south.

The strong influence of the Moorish occupation also shows itself in cooking styles, notably in the use of those wonderful spices saffron, cumin and cinnamon and, of course, in the use of rice. The products imported from the Americas widened the range of beans available, and introduced peppers and potatoes, while the strong Jewish tradition in the country gave yet more elements to absorb into the culinary traditions.

This selection of recipes will give you just a glimpse of the range and variety of Spanish dishes and enable you to enjoy those dishes at home. Use the very freshest, best quality ingredients, cook with care and enthusiasm and you will bring a taste of Spain into your kitchen!

Ingredients

Most of the ingredients used in the recipes are readily available in supermarkets. For a few, you may have to shop at a delicatessen or continental suppliers but there are easy-to-find alternatives which will still give you delicious results.

Chorizo
These garlic and paprika-spiced sausages are now readily available in supermarkets and delicatessens.

Ham
The most famous Spanish ham is *jamon Serrano*, a salt-cured raw ham which is served thinly sliced as an aperitif or added to many dishes for flavour. If you cannot find it, substitute Italian *prosciutto crudo* or German Westphalian ham. In cooking, unsmoked gammon or lean bacon also make an acceptable substitute.

Morcilla
This Spanish black pudding is not always easy to find outside Spain, but any firm black pudding or even a sausage such as kabanos can be substituted.

Olive Oil

The only oil for cooking in a truly authentic Spanish style is olive oil. The finest oils are labelled 'extra virgin' olive oil, but you can experiment to discover which type you prefer. Lard is sometimes used in Spanish cookery from the inland regions.

Peppers

In Spain, a whole variety of peppers of different shapes, sizes and flavours are used in the kitchen. In this book, we have concentrated on those which are readily available. Where roast and skinned peppers are required, you can use canned pimentos if you do not have the time to prepare fresh peppers.

Pulses

Many pulses are used in Spanish cookery, such as dried beans and chick peas. They should be soaked overnight in cold water then drained and boiled for 10 minutes before cooking for about 1½ hours until tender.

Rice

For dishes such as paella, use a medium-grain rice. Italian risotto rice is ideal.

Saffron

Saffron strands are one of the most expensive spices but are required only in very small quantities and really have no substitute. Crush them in a mortar then dissolve in a little warm water or stock before adding to a dish.

Sausages

The most famous Spanish sausages are *butifarra*. They are sometimes available in delicatessens, otherwise you can substitute bratwurst or black pudding, as indicated in the recipe.

Shellfish

The Spaniards love shellfish of all kinds: mussels, prawns, clams and scallops. Always buy them very fresh and use them on the day you purchase. Wash and scrub them well, discarding any which do not close when tapped. Once cooked, discard any which do not open.

Spaniards would always use uncooked prawns for the best flavour and these can be found in fishmongers and good supermarkets. Simply cook them until they turn pink. If you use the more readily-available cooked, peeled prawns, add them at the end of cooking and allow them just to heat through.

Tomatoes

Fresh, ripe tomatoes are a common ingredient in Spanish cookery. You will obtain the best results with large, ripe, full-flavoured tomatoes. Out of season, you will probably be best to use canned tomatoes rather than the often pale and flavourless ones on sale.

If a recipe calls for sieved tomatoes, you can either skin and sieve fresh tomatoes; sieve canned tomatoes; or use canned ready-sieved tomatoes, passata.

Equipment

As with most international cuisine, there are traditional utensils which are tailor-made for particular dishes, although a reasonably-equipped kitchen will offer a range of substitutes and you can use whichever equipment you have to hand.

Cazuela

This is one of the most popular cooking vessels in Spain and is an earthenware casserole, glazed on the inside, used for cooking both on the hob and in the oven, and also for serving. Any earthenware pots should be used with a diffuser on a hob and never placed directly over a high heat or on a cold surface when hot. If you do not have a traditional earthenware pot, use any flameproof casserole dish.

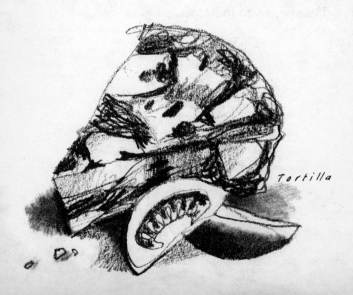

Tortilla

Cooking Methods

There are particular cooking methods used in Spanish cookery, which require practice and experience. In these recipes, you can understand the relevant techniques by following the instructions in the methods. There is nothing which is beyond the capabilities of the ordinary, interested home cook.

Often, the first stage of cooking a dish is to fry the onions to a soft, almost sauce-like consistency before proceeding with the rest of the recipe. Also, meats and vegetables are usually browned separately before wine or stock is added in which to cook them.

One common thickening and flavouring sauce used is a combination of crushed garlic, salt and almonds, sometimes with breadcrumbs. This gives a very distinctive flavour to many Spanish dishes.

Peppers are often roasted before being added to recipes, and the technique of roasting and skinning them is described in the relevant recipes.

Notes on the Recipes

1. Follow one set of measurements only, do not mix metric and Imperial.

2. Eggs are size 2.

3. Wash fresh produce before preparation.

4. Spoon measurements are level.

5. Adjust seasoning and strongly-flavoured ingredients, such as onions and garlic, to suit your own taste.

6. If you substitute dried for fresh herbs, use only half the amount specified.

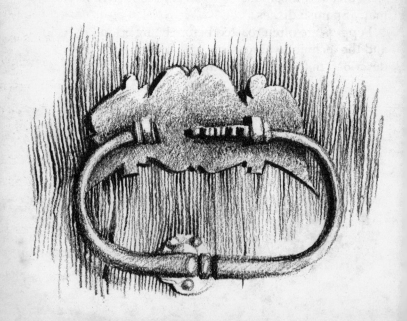

Tapas and Appetisers

Tapas in Spain are not just food, they are a way of life. Spaniards meet in a tapas bar to enjoy the company of friends, lively conversation, a glass or two or sherry and a whole selection of bite-sized pieces of food ranging from simple slivers of ham and cheese to vegetable fritters, roasted peppers or prawns sizzled with garlic. The quantities they eat may seem enough for a whole meal, but serve only as a prelude to a full meal later on!

1 | Figs with Ham

Ingredients

100 g/4 oz Serrano ham or cured ham
8 fresh, ripe figs

Method

1. Cut the ham into thin slices. Peel and quarter the figs.

2. Arrange the fish on serving plates and top with the ham slices.

Serves 4

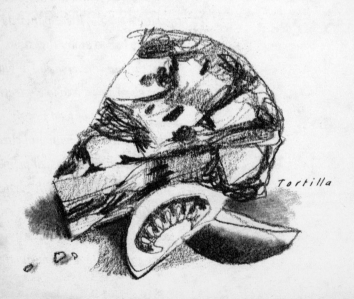

Tortilla

2 Marinated Olives

Ingredients

225 g/8 oz green olives
2 cloves garlic, cut into slivers
1 tsp chopped fresh thyme
1 tsp chopped fresh fennel
½ lemon, cut into thin wedges
Salt
45 ml/3 tbsp olive oil

Method

1. Rinse the olives and drain them well.

2. Place in a screw-top jar with the garlic, thyme, fennel and lemon and sprinkle with salt.

3. Add enough water just to cover the olives. Pour on the olive oil, cover and leave to marinate for 1 week before serving.

Serves 4

3 Marinated Sardines

Ingredients

450 g/1 lb fresh sardines or anchovies
300 ml/½ pt/1¼ cups white wine vinegar
5 ml/1 tsp salt
½ lettuce, shredded
45 ml/3 tbsp olive oil
4 cloves garlic, crushed
30 ml/2 tbsp chopped fresh parsley
1 lemon, sliced
½ onion, cut into rings

Method

1. Cut off the heads, cut the fish and remove the backbones. Arrange the washed fillets in a single layer in a dish.

2. Pour over enough wine vinegar just to cover the fish then sprinkle with salt. Cover and leave to marinate for 12 to 24 hours or until the fish are pale and solid.

3. Drain the fish well and rinse in iced water.

4. Arrange the lettuce on the base of a serving dish. Lay the fish on top. Mix together the oil, garlic and parsley and drizzle over the fish. Serve garnished with lemon slices and onion rings.

Serves 4

4 | Kidneys in Sherry

Ingredients

450 g/1 lb lambs' or calves' kidneys
Salt
60 ml/4 tbsp olive oil
2 onions, chopped
2 cloves garlic, crushed
15 ml/1 tbsp plain flour
1 bay leaf
2.5 ml/½ tsp dried thyme
120 ml/4 fl oz/½ cup dry sherry
120 ml/4 fl oz/½ cup stock
Freshly ground black pepper
30 ml/2 tbsp chopped fresh parsley

Method

1. Wash the kidneys, remove the membrane, cut in half and cut out the core. Soak in salted water for 1 hour. Drain well and cut into cubes.

2. Heat the oil and fry the kidneys for a few minutes then remove from the pan.

3. Add the onions and garlic and fry until softened, stirring frequently. Stir in the flour, bay leaf, thyme and stock and season with salt and pepper. Bring to the boil then simmer until thickened.

4. Return the kidneys to the heat and simmer very gently for about 10 minutes without allowing the sauce to boil. Check and adjust the seasoning to taste then serve sprinkled with parsley.

Serves 4 to 6

5 Meatballs with Almond Sauce

Ingredients

450 g/1 lb minced pork
50 g/2 oz fresh breadcrumbs
2 cloves garlic, crushed
1 onion, finely chopped
30 ml/2 tbsp chopped fresh parsley
Salt and freshly ground black pepper
Pinch of freshly grated nutmeg
1 egg, beaten
Flour for dusting
60 ml/4 tbsp olive oil

For the sauce:
45 ml/3 tbsp olive oil
100 g/4 oz almonds
1 slice bread, diced
2 cloves garlic, crushed
8 black peppercorns
Few strands of saffron
2.5 ml/½ tsp salt
100 ml/3½ fl oz/6½ tbsp dry white wine
300 ml/½ pt/1¼ cups stock or water
5 ml/1 tsp lemon juice
15 ml/1 tbsp chopped fresh parsley

Method

1.   Mix together all the meatball ingredients except the flour and oil and knead until smooth. Shape into small walnut-sized balls and roll them in flour.

2. Heat the oil and fry the meatballs over a medium heat until browned on all sides. Remove from the pan and drain well.

3. Meanwhile, heat the oil for the sauce and fry the almonds, bread and garlic until golden. Remove from the pan and crush in a mortar with the peppercorns, saffron and salt. Gradually add the wine and mix to a smooth paste.

4. Stir the almond paste back into the oil in the pan then add the stock or water, bring to the boil and simmer for 2 minutes, stirring.

5. Add the meatballs, cover and simmer for about 25 minutes, adding a little extra water during cooking if necessary.

6. Sprinkle with lemon juice and parsley before serving.

Serves 4

ESPAÑA

6 Garlic Mushrooms

Ingredients

90 ml/6 tbsp olive oil
6 cloves garlic, chopped
1 dried red chilli pepper, seeded and chopped
450 g/1 lb button mushrooms
Salt and freshly ground black pepper
45 ml/3 tbsp chopped fresh parsley

Method

1. Heat the oil and fry the garlic, chilli pepper and mushrooms for about 10 minutes, stirring frequently.

2. Season with salt and pepper, transfer to a warmed serving dish and serve sprinkled with parsley.

Serves 4

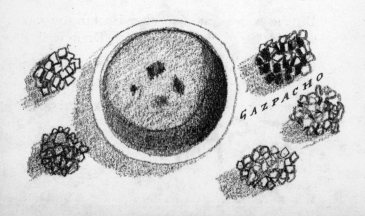

GAZPACHO

7 | Prawns in Overcoats

Ingredients

1 egg
45 ml/3 tbsp water
2.5 ml/½ tsp salt
2.5 ml/½ tsp baking powder
75 g/3 oz/¾ cup plain flour
450 g/1 lb peeled prawns, raw if possible
Oil for deep-frying

For the sauce:
120 ml/4 fl oz/½ cup tomato ketchup
60 ml/4 tbsp mayonnaise
30 ml/2 tbsp white wine vinegar
5 ml/1 tsp paprika
2.5 ml/½ tsp ground cumin
Pinch of cayenne pepper

Method

1. Beat together the egg and water then beat in the salt, baking powder and flour to make a smooth, thick batter. Leave to stand for 1 hour.

2. Dip the prawns into the batter. Heat the oil and deep-fry the prawns until golden. Drain well.

3. Meanwhile, mix together the sauce ingredients, seasoning to taste with cayenne pepper.

4. Spear the prawns with cocktail sticks and serve with the dipping sauce.

Serves 4

8 | Sizzling Prawns

Ingredients

60 ml/4 tbsp olive oil
2 cloves garlic, chopped
Pinch of chilli pepper
Pinch of paprika
225 g/8 oz peeled prawns, raw if possible
Crusty bread

Method

1. Divide the oil between individual ovenproof ramekins. Add the garlic, chilli and paprika. Place the ramekins in a preheated oven at 220°C/425°F/gas mark 7 until the oil is sizzling.

2. Add the prawns, stir well and return to the oven for about 5 minutes until the prawns are hot and the sauce sizzling.

3. Serve with chunks of bread for dipping into the sauce.

Serves 4

9 Fried Scallops

Ingredients

16–24 scallops, shelled
45 ml/3 tbsp plain flour
Salt and freshly ground black pepper
1 egg, beaten
100 g/4 oz breadcrumbs
60 ml/4 tbsp olive oil
1 lemon, cut into wedges

Method

1. Clean the scallops and pat dry. Season the flour with salt and pepper then toss the scallops in the flour, shaking off any excess. Coat in beaten egg then in breadcrumbs.

2. Heat the oil and fry the scallops for about 1 minute on each side until crisp and golden. Serve in scallop shells or small dishes, garnished with the lemon wedges.

Serves 4

10 Fried Squid Rings

Ingredients

450 g/1 lb squid
Flour for dusting
Oil for deep-frying
Salt
1 lemon, cut into wedges

Method

1. Clean the squid and pull the body from the tentacles. Cut off the tentacles and discard the body and innards. Remove the outer membrane and the plastic-like quill. Cut the body into rings.

2. Wash the squid and pat it dry on kitchen paper. Dust it with flour seasoned with salt and shake off any excess.

3. Heat the oil and deep-fry the squid for a few minutes until crisp and golden. Remove and drain well, sprinkle with salt and serve with lemon wedges.

Serves 4

Soups

Many Spanish soups are meals in themselves – more like thick stews to be served on a cold day with hunks of crusty bread. In contrast, the famous chilled soups are delightful for a refreshing but satisfying lunch on a warm summer day

Cream of Asparagus Soup

Ingredients

450 g/l lb asparagus
50 g/2 oz/¼ cup butter
1 leek, sliced
1 carrot, sliced
60 ml/4 tsp medium-grain rice
1 l/1¾ pts/4¼ cups stock or water
30 ml/2 tbsp chopped fresh parsley
200 ml/7 fl oz/scant 1 cup milk
Salt and freshly ground black pepper
Pinch of cayenne pepper
60 ml/4 tbsp single cream

Method

1.   Reserve the asparagus tips; peel and slice the stalks. Melt the butter and fry the stalks, leek and carrot for 20 minutes, covered then stir in the rice.

2.   Meanwhile, cook the asparagus tips for about 7 minutes in the stock or water. Drain and reserve the asparagus and stock.

3.   When the rice has absorbed the liquid in the pan, add the stock and simmer for 30 minutes until tender.

4.   Purée the soup or rub it through a sieve then return it to the pan. Reheat gently, adding the asparagus tips and seasoning with salt, pepper and cayenne pepper. Thin with cream and serve hot or cold.

Serves 4

2 Chick Pea Soup

Ingredients

450 g/1 lb chick peas
5 ml/1 tsp bicarbonate of soda
1.2 l/2 pts/5 cups water
1 onion
1 leek
1 bay leaf
1 sprig fresh parsley
1 sprig fresh thyme
6 eggs, beaten
50 g/2 oz butter, cut into pieces
Salt and freshly ground black pepper

Method

1. Soak the chick peas overnight in cold water with the bicarbonate of soda.

2. Drain the chick peas well and place them in a saucepan with the water, onion, leek, bay leaf, parsley and thyme. Bring to the boil and boil rapidly for 10 minutes. Reduce the heat, cover and simmer for about 2 hours until the chick peas are soft.

3. Remove the vegetables and herbs. Purée the chick peas and stock or rub them through a sieve then return them to the pan over a very low heat.

4. Stir the eggs and butter into the soup and season to taste with salt and pepper. Thin the soup down, if necessary, with a little hot water before serving.

Serves 4

3   Garlic Soup

Ingredients

90 ml/6 tbsp olive oil
6 cloves garlic, chopped
6 slices bread, cubed
5 ml/1 tsp paprika
1.2 l/2 pts/5 cups stock or water, boiling
10 ml/2 tsp salt
4 eggs
30 ml/2 tbsp chopped fresh parsley

Method

1.   Heat the oil in a large flameproof casserole or pan and fry the garlic and bread until lightly browned.

2.   Stir in the paprika then add the boiling stock or water. Return to the boil, cover and simmer for about 20 minutes until the bread has almost disintegrated.

3.   Spoon the soup into warmed individual bowls and break one egg into each bowl. Poach the eggs in the soup on the top of the oven or in a preheated oven at 180°C/350°F/gas mark 4 for a few minutes until the whites are just set. Serve sprinkled with parsley.

Serves 4

4 Granada Soup

Ingredients

75 ml/5 tbsp olive oil
4 onions, chopped
2 green peppers, chopped
3 tomatoes, skinned
4 cloves garlic
Few strands of saffron
4 black peppercorns
1.75 l/3 pts/7½ cups water or stock
Salt and freshly ground black pepper
3 slices bread, diced

Method

1. Heat the oil and fry the onions, peppers and tomatoes for about 10 minutes until soft but not browned.

2. Meanwhile, roast the garlic in a preheated oven at 200°C/400°F/gas mark 6 for about 10 minutes. Remove from the oven and pound to a paste with the saffron and peppercorns.

3. Add the garlic paste to the vegetables. Stir in the water or stock, bring to the boil and simmer for about 20 minutes. Season to taste with salt and pepper.

4. Arrange the bread in the bottom of a warmed soup tureen or individual dishes. Pour over the hot soup and serve.

Serves 4

5 Lentil Soup

Ingredients

450 g/1 lb green lentils
3 l/5¼ pts/12¾ cups water
90 ml/6 tbsp olive oil
1 tomato, skinned and chopped
1 green pepper, diced
1 onion, quartered
1 bay leaf
6 cloves garlic
Salt
2 potatoes, chopped
5 ml/1 tsp paprika
Pinch of cayenne pepper
225 g/8 oz chorizo sausage
Freshly ground black pepper
30 ml/2 tbsp chopped fresh parsley

Method

1. Place the lentils in a large saucepan and cover with twice their volume of water. Bring to the boil then remove from the heat and leave to soak for 1 hour.

2. Drain the lentils then return to the pan and add the water, oil, tomato, pepper, onion, bay leaf and garlic and season with salt. Bring to the boil, partially cover and simmer for 1 hour.

3. Add the potatoes, paprika, cayenne and sausages, return to the boil, cover and simmer for a further 45 minutes until all the ingredients are tender.

4.   Slice the sausages and return them to the pan.
        Season to taste with salt and pepper and serve
        sprinkled with parsley.

        Serves 4 to 6

6 Iced Melon Soup with Ham

Ingredients

> 1 large ripe honeydew melon
> 50 g/2 oz Serrano or cured ham, shredded

Method

1.   Halve the melon, discard the seeds and scoop the
        flesh into a blender. Purée until smooth then chill
        well.

2.   When ready to serve, spoon into chilled soup
        bowls and garnish with the shreds of ham.

        Serves 4

7 Seafood Soup

Ingredients

900 g/2 lb mixed white fish
900 g/2 lb mixed shellfish such as prawns, mussels,
clams, scallops, crab or lobster, scrubbed
3 l/5¼ pts/12¾ cups water
90 ml/6 tbsp dry white wine
2 onions
1 carrot
1 stalk celery
1 bay leaf
Salt and freshly ground black pepper
60 ml/4 tbsp olive oil
1 clove garlic, crushed
75 ml/5 tbsp brandy
2 slices bread, toasted and cubed
Few strands of saffron
6 black peppercorns
2.5 ml/½ tsp cayenne pepper
300 ml/½ pt/1¼ cups sieved tomatoes
30 ml/2 tbsp chopped fresh parsley

Method

1. Fillet the fish and place the heads, bones and trimmings in a large saucepan.

2. Peel the prawns and place the shells with the fish trimmings.

3. Place the mussels, clams and scallops in a large pan with a little water, cover and steam for about 5 minutes until the shells open. Discard any which do not open. Remove and discard the shells, reserving the flesh and cooking liquor.

4. Halve the lobster, remove the shell and add it to the fish bones then slice the flesh. Remove the meat from the crab and add the shell to the fish bones.

5. Add the water, wine, 1 onion, the carrot, celery and bay leaf to the fish bones and season with salt and pepper. Bring to the boil, skim, partially cover and simmer for 1 hour.

6. Chop the remaining onion. Heat the oil in a flameproof casserole and fry the onion and garlic for a few minutes. Add the fish and fry for a few minutes. Add the prawns, lobster and other shellfish.

7. Pour in the brandy and set it alight. Stir carefully until the flames subside.

8. Crush the toast with the saffron, peppercorns and cayenne. Stir in a little stock to make a smooth paste. Add this to the fish with the sieved tomatoes.

9. Strain the stock and add about 2.25 l/4 pts/10 cups of stock to the fish. Bring to the boil and simmer for 15 minutes. Serve sprinkled with parsley.

Serves 6 to 8

8 Tomato Soup with Figs

Ingredients

75 ml/5 tbsp olive oil
1 onion, chopped
4 cloves garlic, chopped
1 kg/2¼ lb ripe tomatoes, skinned, seeded and chopped
2 bay leaves, crumbled
5 ml/1 tsp sugar
2.5 ml/½ tsp paprika
Salt and freshly ground black pepper
4 slices stale bread
8 ripe figs, halved

Method

1. Heat 45 ml/3 tbsp of oil and fry the onion gently until soft. Add the garlic, tomatoes and bay leaves and simmer for about 30 minutes. Season with sugar, paprika, salt and pepper.

2. Rub the sauce through a sieve then return it to the pan and reheat, stirring in the remaining oil. Do not allow the sauce to boil.

3. Lightly toast the bread and place it in 4 large soup bowls. Pour the soup over the top and serve with the figs.

    Serves 4

9 Gazpacho

Ingredients

2 slices bread
900 g/2 lb ripe tomatoes, skinned
4 cloves garlic
10 ml/2 tsp salt
Pinch of ground cumin
75 ml/5 tbsp olive oil
75 ml/5 tbsp white wine vinegar
600 ml/1 pt/2½ cups water
1 onion, chopped
1 cucumber, chopped
1 green pepper, chopped
1 hard-boiled egg, chopped
Ice cubes

Method

1. Cut the crusts from the bread and soak it in water for 20 minutes. Squeeze out any excess moisture.

2. Place the bread, tomatoes, garlic, salt and cumin in a food processor and process until smooth.

3. With the motor running, gradually add the oil. When it has been absorbed, gradually add the wine vinegar. Transfer the mixture to a soup tureen and stir in the water. Chill thoroughly.

4. Serve garnished with a little of the onion, cucumber and pepper, with the remainder served separately with the hard-boiled egg. Float a few ice cubes in the bowl of soup, if liked.

Serves 4 to 6

10 Chilled Almond Soup

Ingredients

4 slices bread
100 g/4 oz/1 cup almonds
6 cloves garlic
120 ml/4 fl oz/½ cup olive oil
60 ml/4 tbsp white wine vinegar
10 ml/2 tsp salt
1.5 l/2½ pts/6 cups water
225 g/8 oz grapes

Method

1. Cut the crusts from the bread and soak it in water for 20 minutes. Squeeze out any excess moisture.

2. Place the bread in a food processor with the almonds and garlic and process until smooth, adding a little water if necessary.

3. With the motor running, gradually add the oil. When it has been absorbed, add the wine vinegar and salt then the water.

4. Pour the soup into a soup tureen and check and adjust the seasoning as necessary. Chill thoroughly.

5. Stir well before serving garnished with the grapes.

Serves 4

Senafood

fish

Spain has a wonderful
tradition of fish and seafood
cookery and a wealth of recipes
which could fill a book in
themselves. This selection offers
just a glimpse of the range and
variety of dishes.

Bream in Green Sauce

Ingredients

450 g/1 lb fillets of bream or hake
Salt
75 ml/5 tbsp olive oil
3 cloves garlic, chopped
2 leeks, chopped
75 ml/5 tbsp chopped fresh parsley
225 g/8 oz potatoes, sliced
50 g/2 oz frozen peas
Flour for dusting
150 ml/¼ pt/⅔ cup dry white wine

Method

1.   Sprinkle the bream with salt and leave to stand.

2.   Heat the oil in a large flameproof casserole and fry
      the garlic and leeks until softened. Stir in the
      parsley then add the potatoes and enough water
      just to cover the vegetables. Bring to the boil, cover
      and simmer for about 15 minutes until the potatoes
      are almost tender.

3.   Add the peas to the pan. Dust the fish with flour.
      Place them on top of the vegetables and pour over
      the wine. Cover again and simmer for about
      15 minutes until the fish is tender, shaking the pot
      regularly while cooking. Serve from the cooking
      pot.

Serves 4

2 Oven-Baked Bream

Ingredients

1 large bream
Salt
150 ml/¼ pt/¾ cup olive oil
5 cloves garlic, chopped
2 red chilli peppers, chopped
15 ml/1 tbsp white wine vinegar

Method

1. Clean and scale the fish, season it with salt and brush with oil. Place it in a shallow ovenproof dish and bake in a preheated oven at 190°C/375°F/gas mark 5 for 30 minutes.

2. When the fish is almost cooked, heat the remaining oil in a frying pan and fry the garlic and chilli peppers until lightly browned. Remove from the heat and stir in the wine vinegar.

3. Transfer the fish to a warmed serving plate, pour over the sauce and serve at once.

Serves 4

Salt Cod with Biscay Sauce

Ingredients

450 g/1 lb salt cod
150 ml/¼ pt/⅔ pt olive oil
4 cloves garlic, chopped
100 g/4 oz bacon, chopped
3 onions, chopped
15 ml/1 tbsp chopped fresh parsley
15 ml/1 tbsp paprika
3 tomatoes, skinned and chopped
Freshly ground black pepper

Method

1. Soak the salt cod in cold water for 24 hours, changing the water at least 4 times. Remove any bones and scales and cut it into strips.

2. Reserve 30 ml/2 tbsp of oil. Heat the remaining oil in a large flameproof casserole and fry the garlic until softened. Add the cod and simmer for about 25 minutes until softened.

3. Meanwhile, heat the reserved oil in a frying pan and fry the bacon and onions over a low heat until softened. Add the parsley, paprika and tomatoes and simmer gently for about 20 minutes, stirring frequently, until the mixture forms a thick sauce. Add a little water during cooking, if necessary. Purée the sauce and rub it through a sieve if you like a smooth sauce.

4. Pour the sauce over the fish, cover and simmer for a further 30 minutes, adding more water if necessary, until the fish is very tender and the sauce is thick.

Serves 4

4 | Hake Casserole

Ingredients

450 g/1 lb small new potatoes
225 g/8 oz peas
8 asparagus spears
90 ml/6 tbsp olive oil
3 onions, chopped
3 cloves garlic, chopped
6 hake steaks
15 ml/1 tbsp plain flour
150 l/¼ pt/⅔ cup dry white wine
4 slices bread, diced
3 hard-boiled eggs, quartered

Method

1.   Cook the potatoes, peas and asparagus separately in boiling water until tender. Drain well.

2.   Heat 60 ml/4 tbsp of oil in a flameproof casserole and fry the onions and garlic until lightly browned. Add the hake and turn it so that it is coated in the hot oil.

3.   Stir in the flour and cook for 1 minute. Add the wine, bring to the boil, cover and simmer gently for 5 minutes, turning the fish once or twice, until the fish is tender.

4.   Meanwhile, heat the remaining oil and fry the bread dice until lightly browned.

5.   Arrange the hot vegetables on a warm serving plate, place the hake in the centre and spoon over the sauce. Serve garnished with the fried bread and hard-boiled eggs.

Serves 6

5 Monkfish with Clams

Ingredients

90 ml/6 tbsp olive oil
2 onions, chopped
3 cloves garlic, chopped
15 ml/1 tbsp chopped fresh parsley
90 ml/6 tbsp sieved tomatoes
15 ml/1 tbsp paprika
175 ml/6 fl oz/⅔ cup water
Few strands of saffron, crushed
225 g/8 oz peas
200 g/7 oz canned red peppers, drained
900 g/2 lb monkfish, thickly sliced
24 small clams, scrubbed
Salt and freshly ground black pepper

Method

1. Heat the oil in a large flameproof casserole and fry the onions, garlic and parsley until softened.

2. Add the sieved tomatoes and saffron and simmer for 5 minutes. Add the peas and peppers and simmer for 5 minutes. Add the monkfish and clams, season with salt and pepper and simmer over a low heat for about 10 minutes until the clams have opened and the fish is tender. Discard any clams that have not opened. Serve at once.

Serves 4 to 6

6 Granada-Style Sardines

Ingredients

30 ml/2 tbsp olive oil
4 cloves garlic, crushed
450 g/1 lb sardines, cleaned
Juice of ½ lemon
150 ml/¼ pt/⅔ cup dry white wine
15 ml/1 tbsp chopped fresh parsley
Salt and freshly ground black pepper

Method

1. Heat the oil in a flameproof casserole, add the garlic and fry for 30 seconds. Add the remaining ingredients, cover and cook for about 15 minutes, stirring occasionally, until the fish are cooked.

2. Serve piping hot from the cooking dish.

Serves 4

7 Swordfish Kebabs

Ingredients

450 g/1 lb swordfish steaks or other firm-fleshed fish,
cubed
45 ml/3 tbsp olive oil
Juice of 1 lemon
4 cloves garlic, chopped
30 ml/2 tbsp chopped fresh parsley
5 ml/1 tsp salt
Freshly ground black pepper
2 firm tomatoes, cut into wedges
1 onion, cut into wedges
1 green pepper, cut into wedges
1 red pepper, cut into wedges
Alioli Sauce (page 150)

Method

1. Place the fish in a bowl. Mix together the oil, lemon juice, garlic, parsley, salt and pepper and pour the mixture over the fish. Stir gently then leave to marinate for 45 minutes.

2. Remove the fish from the marinade and thread it on to skewers, alternating with the tomatoes, onion and peppers. Season lightly with salt and pepper and brush with a little of the marinade.

3. Grill the kebabs under a hot grill or on a barbecue, turning frequently and basting with the marinade as they cook.

Serves 4

8 Sole with Basque Sauce

Ingredients

450 g/1 lb potatoes, sliced
900 g/2 lb sole
Juice of ½ lemon
Salt and freshly ground black pepper
25 g/1 oz butter
15 ml/1 tbsp olive oil

For the sauce:
25 g/1 oz butter
1 small onion, chopped
100 g/4 oz mushrooms, chopped
2 red peppers, chopped
150 l/¼ pt/⅔ cup sieved tomatoes

Method

1.   Arrange the potatoes on the base of a greased, shallow ovenproof dish. Bake in a preheated oven at 180°C/350°F/gas mark 4 for 15 minutes.

2.   Place the sole on top of the potatoes and sprinkle with lemon juice, salt and pepper. Dot with the butter and sprinkle with the oil. Return to the oven for a further 20 minutes until the fish is cooked.

3.   Drain the liquid from the fish and reserve it for the sauce. Fillet the fish, then arrange the fillets back in the dish and keep them warm.

4. Meanwhile, melt the butter for the sauce and fry the onion, mushrooms and pepper until soft. Add the sieved tomatoes and the liquid from the fish and season with salt and pepper. Simmer until thickened slightly.

5. Pour the sauce over the fish and return it to the oven for about 15 minutes. Serve from the cooking dish.

Serves 4

Santiago de Compostela

FRANCE

PORTUGAL

Valladolid

Madrid

Barcelona

SPAIN

Valencia

MALLORCA

Seville

IBIZA

MENORCA

Granada

Alicante

Malaga

Almeria

Gibraltar

MOROCCO

ALGERIA

9 | Salmon in Cider

Ingredients

15 ml/1 tbsp butter
15 ml/1 tbsp olive oil
100 g/4 oz Serrano or cured ham, thinly sliced
30 ml/2 tbsp plain flour
Freshly ground black pepper
4 salmon steaks
175 ml/6 fl oz/¾ cup dry cider
120 ml/4 fl oz/½ cup stock or cider

Method

1. Heat the butter and oil and fry the ham briefly then remove from the pan.

2. Season the flour with pepper and dust the salmon in the flour. Add them to the pan and fry until lightly coloured on both sides.

3. Transfer the salmon to a warm ovenproof dish into which they just fit then arrange the ham in the spaces around them.

4. Add 15 ml/1 tbsp of the flour to the juices in the pan and stir well for 1 minute. Stir in the cider and bring to the boil, stirring then pour the juices over the fish. Top up with a little stock or more cider so that the fish is almost covered with liquid. Cover and cook in a preheated oven at 200°C/400°F/gas mark 6 for 15 minutes.

Serves 4

10 | Trout with Ham

Ingredients

4 trout, cleaned
Salt
175 g/6 oz Serrano ham or cured ham
4 cloves garlic
Flour for dusting
15 ml/1 tbsp chopped fresh parsley
5 ml/1 tsp thyme
Freshly ground black pepper
75 ml/5 tbsp olive oil
1 lemon, cut into wedges

Method

1. Sprinkle the trout with salt inside and out. Place a slice of ham and a clove of garlic inside the cavity of each fish. Season the flour with parsley, thyme and pepper. Dust the fish in the flour and shake off any excess.

2. Heat the oil in a large frying pan and add the fish in a single layer. Fry until crisp and brown on the underside then turn and fry the other side. Serve garnished with lemon wedges.

Serves 4

11 | Basque Tuna Stew

Ingredients

1 dried red chilli pepper
3 cloves garlic
90 ml/6 tbsp olive oil
1 green pepper, cut into strips
2 onions, chopped
4 ripe tomatoes, skinned and chopped
900 g/2 lb potatoes, cut into chunks
15 ml/1 tbsp brandy
Salt
900 g/2 lb tuna fillet, cut into pieces

Method

1. Soak the chilli pepper in warm water for 2 hours then drain. Grind to a paste with the garlic.

2. Heat the oil in a large flameproof casserole. Add the pepper, onions and tomatoes and fry over a low heat until tender. Stir in the chilli and garlic paste.

3. Add the potatoes and brandy and stir in just enough water to cover the ingredients. Season with salt, cover and simmer for about 30 minutes until the potatoes are tender.

4. Add the tuna, cover and simmer for about 10 minutes until the fish is cooked. Leave to stand for 10 minutes before serving.

Serves 4 to 6

12 Spanish-Style King Prawns

Ingredients

45 ml/3 tbsp olive oil
1 onion, chopped
2 cloves garlic, chopped
1 bay leaf, crumbled
15 ml/1 tbsp chopped fresh parsley
90 ml/6 tbsp dry white wine
450 g/1 lb raw, unpeeled king prawns

Method

1. Heat the oil and fry the onion and garlic until softened. Add the bay leaf and parsley and fry for 3 minutes.

2. Add the wine and prawns, bring to a simmer, cover and simmer gently for about 20 minutes until the prawns are cooked.

Serves 4

ESPAÑA

13 Stuffed Squid in Black Sauce

Ingredients

450 g/1 lb squid
60 ml/4 tbsp fine breadcrumbs
2 cloves garlic, chopped
Flour for dusting
75 ml/5 tbsp olive oil
1 onion, chopped
4 tomatoes, skinned and chopped
120 ml/4 fl oz/½ cup dry white wine
1 bay leaf
Salt and freshly ground black pepper
Pinch of cayenne pepper
15 ml/1 tbsp chopped fresh parsley

Method

1. Clean the squid and pull the body from the tentacles. Reserve the ink sacs. Cut off the tentacles and discard the body and innards. Remove the outer membrane and the plastic-like quill.

2. Finely chop the tentacles and mix them with the breadcrumbs and 1 clove of garlic. Use this mixture to stuff the squid and close the tops with cocktail sticks. Dust lightly with flour.

3. Heat the oil and fry the squid until lightly browned. Transfer to a flameproof casserole.

4.   Reheat the oil and fry the onion and remaining garlic until soft. Add the tomatoes and fry for a few minutes. Add the wine, bay leaf, salt, pepper and cayenne pepper and simmer, stirring frequently, for 15 minutes.

5.   Crush the ink sacs then stir them into the sauce. Simmer for a further 15 minutes. Sieve the sauce if you like a smooth sauce, then pour it over the squid in the casserole. Cover and simmer gently for about 25 minutes until the squid is tender, adding a little more liquid to the sauce during cooking if necessary. Serve garnished with parsley.

Serves 4

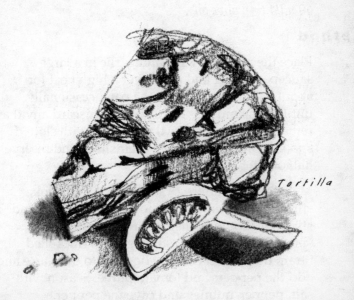

Tortilla

14 | Stuffed Mussels

Ingredients

675 g/1½ lb mussels, scrubbed and bearded
30 ml/2 tbsp dry white wine
1 clove garlic, chopped
75 g/3 oz/⅓ cup butter
45 ml/3 tbsp plain flour
250 ml/8 fl oz/1 cup milk, hot
15 ml/1 tbsp chopped red pepper
15 ml/1 tbsp chopped green pepper
5 ml/1 tsp tomato purée
Salt and freshly ground black pepper
Freshly grated nutmeg
Pinch of cayenne pepper
100 g/4 oz breadcrumbs
60 ml/4 tbsp olive oil

Method

1. Place the mussels, wine and garlic in a large saucepan, cover and cook over a high heat for about 5 minutes, shaking the pan occasionally, until all the mussels have opened; discard any that remain closed. Remove the mussels with slotted spoon, remove them from their shells and reserve half of the biggest shells.

2. Melt half the butter, stir in the flour and cook, stirring, for 1 minute. Remove from the heat and stir in the hot milk then return to the heat and simmer for 3 minutes, stirring, until thickened. Strain the mussel cooking liquid into the sauce and add the peppers and tomato purée. Season with salt, pepper, nutmeg and cayenne pepper.

3.   Chop the mussels into 2 or 3 pieces and add them to the sauce. Spoon them into the reserved mussel shells.

4.   Heat the remaining butter with the oil and fry the breadcrumbs until crisp. Sprinkle over the mussels then brown them under a hot grill for a few minutes before serving.

Serves 4

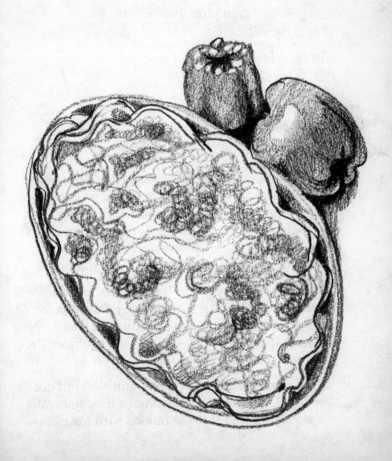

15 | Clam Empanada

Ingredients

15 g/½ oz fresh yeast
5 ml/1 tsp caster sugar
225 g/8 oz polenta
200 ml/7 fl oz/scant 1 cup warm water
30 ml/2 tbsp olive oil
2 eggs, beaten
250 g/9 oz/2¼ cups plain flour
5 ml/1 tsp salt

For the filling:
900 g/2 lb clams, scrubbed
45 ml/3 tbsp olive oil
3 onions chopped
Few strands of saffron, crushed

Method

1.   Mix together the sugar and yeast. Place the polenta in a bowl and work in the water, oil and eggs then beat in the yeast mixture. Gradually add the flour and salt and knead until the dough is smooth, soft and no longer sticky. Cover and leave in a warm place for about 30 minutes.

2.   To make the filling, place the clams in a large saucepan with a little water. Cover and cook over a high heat for about 4 minutes until the clams open; discard any that remain closed. Remove from the pan and shell the clams.

3.   Heat the oil and fry the onions until soft but not browned. Dissolve the saffron in a little hot water or stock then add it to the onions with the clams.

4. Divide the dough in half and roll out on a lightly floured surface into a large rectangle. Place on a greased baking sheet. Spread the filling over the dough, leaving a gap round the edge. Roll out the remaining dough, damp the edges and seal on top of the first sheet. Roll out the trimmings and use to decorate the top. Brush with a little oil and prick the top a few times with a fork.

5. Bake in a preheated oven at 200°C/400°F/gas mark 6 for about 20 minutes until golden brown. Serve hot or cold, cut into squares.

Serves 8

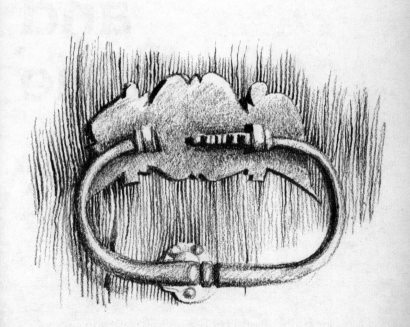

Poultry and Game

Chicken is popular throughout Spain, and there are many game dishes which originate in the interior of the country.

1 Garlic Chicken with Sherry

Ingredients

1 chicken, cut into pieces
5 ml/1 tsp paprika
Salt and freshly ground black pepper
90 ml/6 tbsp olive oil
10 cloves garlic, chopped
15 ml/1 tbsp brandy
120 ml/4 fl oz/½ cup dry sherry
2 bay leaves

Method

1. Rub the chicken portions with paprika, salt and pepper.

2. Heat the oil in a large flameproof casserole and fry the garlic until lightly browned then remove it from the pan. Add the chicken portions and fry until lightly browned on all sides. Return the garlic to the pan and add the brandy, sherry and bay leaves. Bring to the boil, cover and simmer for about 40 minutes until the chicken is tender.

Serves 4

2 Chicken with Almond Sauce

Ingredients

4 chicken portions
Salt and freshly ground black pepper
60 ml/4 tbsp olive oil
6 cloves garlic, crushed
20 almonds
Pinch of ground cinnamon
15 ml/1 tbsp chopped fresh parsley
2 cloves
6 black peppercorns
Few strands of saffron, crushed
5 ml/1 tsp salt
1 onion, chopped
45 ml/3 tbsp water
300 ml/½ pt/1¼ cups dry white wine
2 bay leaves

Method

1.   Season the chicken with salt and pepper. Heat the oil and fry 4 cloves of garlic with the almonds until golden brown. Transfer to a blender and purée with the cinnamon, parsley, cloves, peppercorns, saffron and salt, adding a little water to make a smooth paste.

2.   Reheat the oil and fry the chicken with the onion until lightly browned. Add the almond paste with the remaining water, wine and bay leaves. Bring to the boil, cover and simmer for about 50 minutes until the chicken is very tender, adding a little more water during cooking if necessary.

Serves 4

3 Chicken with Olives

Ingredients

4 boned chicken breasts
Salt and freshly ground black pepper
75 ml/4 tbsp olive oil
12 black or green olives, stoned and chopped
1 onion, finely chopped
15 ml/1 tbsp chopped fresh parsley
2.5 ml/½ tsp paprika
15 ml/1 tbsp white wine vinegar

Method

1. Cut the chicken breasts in half horizontally and brush generously with olive oil. Season with salt and pepper. Grill under a hot grill for about 10 minutes until tender and cooked through, brushing with a little more olive oil during cooking if necessary.

2. Mix the olives with the onion, parsley, paprika and wine vinegar and season with salt and pepper.

3. Transfer the chicken to a warm serving plate, spoon over the sauce and serve hot or cold.

Serves 4

4 Chicken with Red Peppers

Ingredients

1 chicken, cut into pieces
Salt and freshly ground black pepper
5 red peppers
75 ml/5 tbsp olive oil
5 cloves garlic, chopped
225 g/8 oz Serrano ham or cured ham
2 onions, chopped
4 tomatoes, skinned and chopped

Method

1. Rub the chicken with salt and pepper.

2. Place the peppers under a grill and grill, turning frequently, until the skins are charred. Remove from the grill and place in a plastic bag. Leave until sufficiently cooled to cut off and discard the stem and seeds and peel away the skin. Cut the pepper into strips.

3. Heat the oil in a flameproof casserole and fry the chicken portions until lightly browned. Add the garlic, ham and onions and fry until the onion is beginning to soften. Add the pepper and tomatoes, cover and simmer for about 30 minutes until the chicken is tender and the sauce is thick.

Serves 4

5 Chicken in Wine Sauce

Ingredients

60 ml/4 tbsp olive oil
1 onion, chopped
2 cloves garlic, chopped
1 bouquet garni
4 chicken portions
15 ml/1 tbsp plain flour
300 ml/½ pt/1¼ cups dry white wine
200 g/7 oz canned pimentos, cut into strips
Few strands of saffron
Freshly grated nutmeg
Salt and freshly ground black pepper
4 slices bread, cut into triangles

Method

1. Heat half the oil in a flameproof casserole and fry the onion and garlic until soft but not browned. Add the bouquet garni and chicken and fry for about 20 minutes until browned on all sides.

2. Sprinkle on the flour and fry, stirring, for 1 minute. Add the wine and pimentos and bring to the boil. Stir in the saffron and season with nutmeg, salt and pepper. Simmer gently for about 20 minutes until the chicken is very tender and the sauce has reduced.

3. Meanwhile, heat the remaining oil and fry the bread until crisp. Arrange round the top of the casserole and serve from the cooking dish.

Serves 4

6 | Paprika Chicken

Ingredients

1 chicken
15 ml/1 tbsp paprika
Salt and freshly ground black pepper
45 ml/3 tbsp olive oil
9 cloves garlic, unpeeled and smashed
2 dried red chilli pepper, seeded and chopped
300 ml/½ pt/1¼ cups chicken stock
Few strands of saffron, crumbled
Pinch of freshly grated nutmeg
50 g/2 oz almonds, toasted
15 ml/1 tbsp pine nuts, toasted
30 ml/2 tbsp chopped fresh parsley
15 ml/1 tsp lemon juice
Pinch of sugar

Method

1. Cut the chicken into bite-sized pieces and season with paprika, salt and pepper.

2. Heat the oil in a flameproof casserole and fry the garlic until lightly browned. Reserve 4 fried cloves. Add the chicken and fry over a high heat until lightly browned then remove from the pan and reserve. Pour off all but 15 ml/1 tbsp of oil. Add the chilli peppers, stir well then add the stock, saffron and nutmeg, bring to the boil and simmer for 2 minutes. Return the chicken to the casserole.

3. Peel the reserved garlic and pound to a paste with a pinch of salt, the almonds, pine nuts and parsley. Work in a little of the stock then stir the mixture into the casserole with the lemon juice and sugar. Simmer gently for 15 minutes. Check and adjust the seasoning before serving.

Serves 4

7 Chicken with Prawns

Ingredients

1 chicken
Salt and freshly ground black pepper
75 ml/5 tbsp olive oil
450 g/1 lb raw, unpeeled prawns
60 ml/4 tbsp Pernod
1 onion, chopped
4 cloves garlic, chopped
450 g/1 lb ripe tomatoes, skinned, seeded and chopped
1 bouquet garni
150 ml/¼ pt/½ cup dry white wine
120 ml/4 fl oz/½ cup chicken stock or water
25 g/1 oz/¼ cup almonds, toasted
3 plain biscuits
30 ml/2 tbsp chopped fresh parsley

Method

1. Cut the chicken into bite-sized pieces, discarding the skin and bones, and season with salt and pepper.

2. Heat 30 ml/2 tbsp of oil in a flameproof casserole and fry the prawns for about 4 minutes until pink. Transfer them to a warm dish. Warm the Pernod and spoon it over the prawns then ignite it. Let the flames die away then reserve the prawns.

3. Heat the remaining oil and fry the onion and chicken for a few minutes, stirring constantly. Add half the garlic and fry until everything is lightly browned. Add the tomatoes and bouquet garni and simmer until the mixture thickens to a sauce.

4. Add the wine with enough stock or water just to cover the chicken. Bring to the boil, cover and simmer for 20 minutes.

5. Pound the remaining garlic with a little salt then work in the almonds and biscuits. Work in the parsley.

6. Discard the bouquet garni and work the seasoning paste into the sauce. Peel the prawns if you prefer then return the prawns to the pan and allow them to heat through. Check and adjust the seasoning before serving.

Serves 4

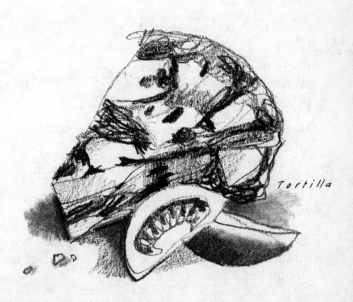

Tortilla

8 Quail with Olives

Ingredients

12 quail
Salt and freshly ground black pepper
90 ml/6 tbsp olive oil
3 cloves garlic, chopped
1 onion, chopped
100 g/4 oz Serrano or cured ham, chopped
3 carrots, diced
30 ml/2 tbsp plain flour
900 ml/1½ pts/3¾ cups chicken stock, boiling
2.5 ml/½ tsp thyme
15 ml/1 tbsp chopped fresh parsley
2 bay leaves
175 g/6 oz olives, stoned

Method

1. Clean the quail, tuck the wing tips underneath the body and tie the legs together. Season with salt and pepper.

2. Heat the oil in a flameproof casserole. Add the quail and fry until lightly browned on all sides. Remove from the pan. Add the garlic and onion and fry until lightly browned. Add the ham and cook for 3 minutes then add the carrots and cook for 4 minutes.

3. Sprinkle in the flour and cook, stirring, for a few minutes. Add the hot stock, cover and simmer for 20 minutes.

4.   Return the quail to the pan, add the thyme, parsley and bay leaves and simmer, uncovered, for 15 minutes, stirring frequently.

5.   Just before serving, add the olives, bring to the boil and boil for 3 minutes. Transfer the quail to a warmed serving plate, spoon over the sauce and serve very hot.

Serves 4

9 | Rabbit with Potatoes

Ingredients

> 2 rabbits, divided into portions
> 250 ml/8 fl oz/1 cup water
> 30 ml/2 tbsp white wine vinegar
> 60 ml/4 tbsp Spanish brandy
> 90 ml/6 tbsp olive oil
> Salt and freshly ground black pepper
> 2 sprigs fresh thyme
> 1 bay leaf
> 450 g/1 lb onions, sliced
> 4 cloves garlic, chopped
> 400 g/14 oz canned tomatoes
> 250 ml/8 fl oz/1 cup red wine
> 600 g/1¼ lb potatoes

Method

1. Soak the rabbit in the water and wine vinegar overnight. Drain and pat dry. Place in a shallow bowl and sprinkle with brandy. Leave to marinate for at least 2 hours.

2. Heat the oil in a large frying pan. Season the rabbit pieces with salt and pepper and fry for about 20 minutes until golden on all sides. Transfer to an ovenproof casserole dish, pour in any remaining marinade and add the thyme and bay leaf.

3. Add the onions to the frying pan and fry until soft. Add the garlic, tomatoes and wine and heat through, stirring to break up the tomatoes. Bring to the boil then pour over the rabbit. Cover and cook in a preheated oven at 180°C/350°F/gas mark 4 for about 1 hour until the rabbit is tender.

4. Cut the potatoes into chip shapes and add to the casserole, pushing them under the sauce. Return to the oven for a further 30 minutes or until the potatoes are tender.

Serves 6

10 Venison with Raisins and Pine Nuts

Ingredients

450 g/1 lb venison steaks, cut into pieces
600 ml/1 pt/2½ cups milk
45 ml/3 tbsp raisins
75 ml/5 tbsp brandy
120 ml/4 fl oz/½ cup olive oil
1 onion, chopped
4 cloves
2 sprigs fresh thyme
2.5 ml/½ tsp oregano
Salt and freshly ground black pepper
1.2 l/2 pts/5 cups chicken stock
60 ml/4 tbsp pine nuts
15 ml/1 tbsp butter
8 small pearl onions

Method

1. Place the venison pieces in a bowl, cover with the milk and leave to stand for 12 hours. Place the raisins and 30 ml/2 tbsp of brandy in a bowl and leave to soak.

2. Drain the meat, pat dry and place in a large flameproof casserole. Place over a very low heat until the meat is dry. Pour in the remaining brandy, heat briefly, ignite it then wait for the flames to die down.

3.   Add the oil, onion, cloves, thyme and oregano and season with salt and pepper. Simmer over a low heat for 5 minutes. Add the stock, bring to the boil, cover and simmer gently for 2 hours.

4.   Drain the raisins and add them to the pot with the pine nuts. Continue to simmer for 10 minutes, shaking the pan frequently.

5.   Meanwhile, melt the butter and gently fry the pearl onions for about 10 minutes until lightly browned.

6.   Transfer the venison to a warm serving plate and surround with the onions. Strain the juice in which the venison as cooked through a sieve and spoon a little over the meat. Serve the remainder separately, if liked.

Serves 4

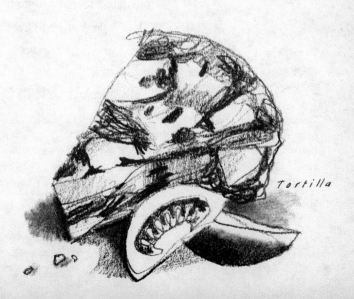

Tortilla

Meat

Lamb is the speciality of central Spain, but all meats are enjoyed throughout the country in a range of recipes from delicious roast lamb to rich pork or beef stews.

1 Lamb Chops with Tomato Sauce

Ingredients

30 ml/2 tbsp olive oil
30 ml/2 tbsp lard
8 lamb chops
2 onions, chopped
50 g/2 oz Serrano or cured ham, chopped
450 g/1 lb tomatoes, skinned, seeded and chopped
Salt and freshly ground black pepper
100 g/4 oz chorizo sausage, sliced

Method

1. Heat the oil and lard and fry the lamb chops until lightly browned on both sides. Transfer them to an ovenproof dish.

2. Add the onions and ham to the pan and fry until soft and lightly browned. Stir in the tomatoes and simmer gently, stirring frequently, until the mixture forms a thick sauce. Season with salt and pepper.

3. Pour the sauce over the chops and arrange the sliced chorizo on top. Cover and bake in a preheated oven at 190°C/375°F/gas mark 5 for about 30 minutes until tender.

Serves 4

2 | Lamb Fricassée

Ingredients

45 ml/3 tbsp olive oil
4 cloves garlic, crushed
450 g/1 lb lean lamb, cubed
2 onions, chopped
5 ml/1 tsp paprika
15 ml/1 tbsp chopped fresh parsley
Juice of ½ lemon
Salt and freshly ground black pepper

Method

1. Heat the oil in a flameproof casserole and fry the garlic until lightly browned. Add the lamb and fry until browned on all sides. Add the onions and fry until softened. Add the paprika, parsley and lemon juice and season with salt and pepper.

2. Cover tightly and simmer very gently for about 45 minutes until the lamb is tender, stirring frequently and adding a little water if necessary during cooking.

   Serves 4

3 Kidneys in Sherry

Ingredients

450 g/1 lb lambs' kidneys
45 ml/3 tbsp olive oil
150 ml/¼ pt/⅔ cup dry sherry
10 ml/2 tsp butter
10 ml/2 tsp plain flour
30 ml/2 tbsp stock
15 ml/1 tbsp chopped fresh parsley
Salt and freshly ground black pepper

Method

1. Clean the kidneys, remove the membrane and cut them in half. Cut out the central core.

2. Heat the oil and fry the kidneys until almost cooked then remove from the pan and slice. Return them to the pan, pour on the sherry, cover and simmer gently for about 2 minutes.

3. Mix together the butter and flour, stir in the stock and stir it into the sherry. Stir in the parsley and season with salt and pepper. Simmer for a few minutes, stirring, until the sauce is clear and thick. Serve at once.

Serves 4

4 Tomato Pork

Ingredients

75 ml/5 tbsp olive oil
450 g/1 lb lean pork, cubed
2 onions, chopped
3 cloves garlic, chopped
450 g/1 lb tomatoes, skinned and chopped
2 bay leaves
5 ml/1 tsp salt
Freshly ground black pepper

Method

1. Heat the oil and fry the pork until lightly browned on all sides. Add the onions and garlic and fry until softened.

2. Add the tomatoes, bay leaves, salt and pepper, bring to the boil, cover and simmer for about 35 minutes, stirring occasionally, until the pork is tender and the sauce is thick.

Serves 4

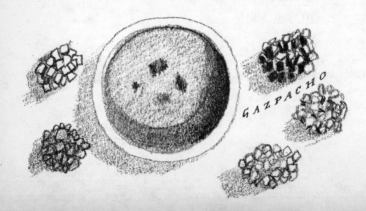

GAZPACHO

5 | Beef with Watercress Sauce

Ingredients

4 rump steaks
Salt and freshly ground black pepper
50 g/2 oz butter
60 ml/4 tbsp Spanish brandy

For the sauce:
15 ml/1 tbsp butter
2 shallots, chopped
150 ml/¼ pt/⅔ cup dry white wine
300 ml/½ pt/1¼ cups stock
1 bunch watercress, chopped
120 ml/4 fl oz/½ cup double cream

Method

1. To make the sauce, melt the butter and fry the shallots until soft. Add the wine, stock and watercress, bring to the boil and simmer until reduced by half.

2. Purée the sauce then return it to the pan, stir in the cream and reduce again until thick. Season to taste with salt and pepper.

3. Meanwhile, season the steaks well with salt and pepper. Heat the butter and fry the steaks until cooked to your taste. Pour over the brandy and ignite it, scooping the juices over the steaks. Serve at once with the sauce.

Serves 4

6 Roast Pork with Caramel Sauce

Ingredients

900 g/2 lb pork loin
45 ml/3 tbsp olive oil
Grated rind of 1 orange
Grated rind of 1 lemon
225 g/8 oz/1 cup sugar
900 ml/1½ pts/3¾ cups milk
450 ml/¾ pt/2 cups water
½ cinnamon stick

For the caramel:
175 g/6 oz/¾ cup sugar
150 ml/¼ pt/⅔ cup water

Method

1. Brush the pork generously with the oil. Place it in a flameproof casserole and fry over a high heat until browned on all sides.

2. Add the orange and lemon rind, the sugar, milk, water and cinnamon, bring to the boil, cover and simmer for about 1½ hours until the pork is tender.

3. Meanwhile, make the caramel. Stir the sugar with half the water until dissolved then boil until the caramel turns light golden. Stir in the remaining water.

4. Remove the pork from the pan when it is tender and keep it warm. Add the caramel into the pan, stir well and simmer over a low heat for about 20 minutes, stirring occasionally, until the liquid is reduced by half.

5. Slice the pork and arrange it on a warmed serving plate. Pour over a little of the sauce and serve the rest separately.

Serves 6

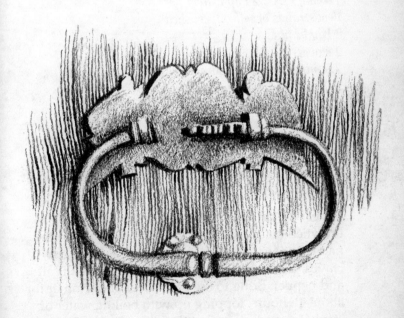

7 Rich Beef Stew

Ingredients

30 ml/2 tbsp olive oil
2 onions, sliced
6 cloves garlic, chopped
2 carrots, sliced
1 green pepper, sliced
450 g/1 lb stewing beef, cubed
2 tomatoes, skinned and chopped
300 ml/½ pt/1¼ cups dry white wine
120 ml/4 fl oz/½ cup water
Few strands of saffron, crushed
3 bay leaves
2 cloves
2.5 ml/½ tsp ground cinnamon
Salt and freshly ground black pepper
225 g/8 oz potatoes, diced

Method

1.   Heat the oil in a large flameproof casserole and fry
      the onions, garlic, carrots and pepper until
      softened. Remove from the pan.

2.   Reheat the oil and fry the beef until lightly
      browned on all sides. Return the vegetables to the
      pan with the tomatoes, wine, water, saffron, bay
      leaves, cloves and cinnamon and season with salt
      and pepper. Bring to the boil, cover and simmer for
      about 1½ hours, topping up with boiling water or
      stock if necessary so that the meat remains just
      covered with the liquid.

3. Add the potatoes and simmer for a further
25 minutes until the meat and all the vegetables
are tender.

Serves 4 to 6

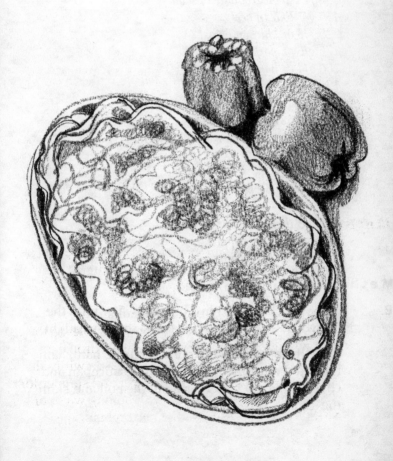

8 Madrid-Style Beef and Chick Peas

Ingredients

450 g/1 lb chick peas
5 ml/1 tsp bicarbonate of soda
450 g/1 lb lean beef
225 g/8 oz chicken breast
175 g/6 oz pork or bacon
100 g/4 oz ham trimmings
1 ham bone
4 beef marrow bones
100 g/4 oz chorizo sausages
100 g/4 oz morcilla or black pudding
3 carrots
3 potatoes
750 g/1½ lb cabbage
Salt
45 ml/3 tbsp olive oil
2 cloves garlic, chopped
225 g/8 oz macheroni

Method

1. Place the chick peas in a bowl of water with the bicarbonate of soda and leave to soak overnight.

2. Place the beef, chicken, pork or bacon, ham, ham bone and marrow bones in a large saucepan and cover with cold water. Bring to the boil and skim the surface.

3.   Drain the chick peas and place them in a square of muslin to keep them separate from the meat. Add to the saucepan, boil for 10 minutes then reduce the heat, cover and simmer for 1 hour.

4.   Add the chorizo and morcilla or black pudding, cover and simmer for 1 hour. Add the carrots, cover and simmer for 30 minutes. Add the potatoes, cover and simmer for 30 minutes.

5.   Meanwhile, boil the cabbage separately in salted water for 30 minutes then drain and cut into pieces. Heat the oil in a frying pan and fry the cabbage and garlic until tender.

6.   Drain the stock from the meats into a large saucepan. Add the macheroni, season with salt, cover and simmer for 20 minutes until tender.

7.   Meanwhile, slice the meats, arrange them on a warm serving plate. Arrange the vegetables on a separate plate and keep them both warm. Serve the stock with the macaroni first, followed by the vegetables and then the meat.

Serves 6 to 8

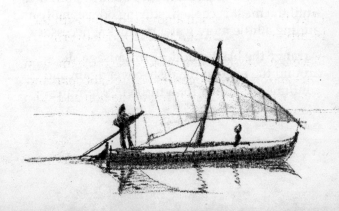

9 Catalan Minced Beef

Ingredients

45 ml/3 tbsp olive oil
450 g/1 lb minced beef
2 onions, chopped
2 tomatoes, skinned and chopped
2 carrots, chopped
15 ml/1 tbsp plain flour
150 ml/¼ pt/⅔ cup stock or water
225 g/8 oz Spanish black pudding or kabanos, sliced
Salt and freshly ground black pepper

Method

1. Heat the oil in a shallow flameproof dish and fry the beef until lightly browned then remove it from the dish.

2. Add the onions, tomatoes and carrots and fry, stirring continuously, for 5 minutes. Stir in the flour and cook, stirring, for 1 minute.

3. Return the meat to the pan with the stock, bring to the boil, cover and simmer for about 40 minutes until the meat is cooked, stirring occasionally and adding a little more water or stock if necessary.

4. Arrange the black pudding or sausage slices around the edge of the dish, cover again and continue to simmer for a further 20 minutes.

Serves 4

10 Seville Veal

Ingredients

45 ml/3 tbsp olive oil
3 cloves garlic, chopped
450 g/1 lb veal fillets
2 onions, chopped
2 carrots, chopped
15 ml/1 tbsp plain flour
600 ml/1 pt/2½ cups stock, hot
150 ml/¼ pt/⅔ cup dry sherry
15 ml/1 tbsp chopped fresh parsley
Salt and freshly ground black pepper
12 olives, stoned

Method

1. Heat the oil in a flameproof casserole and fry the garlic until lightly browned then remove it from the pan. Add the veal and fry until lightly browned then remove it from the pan. Add the onions and carrots and fry until softened.

2. Stir in the flour and cook, stirring, for 1 minute. Stir in the hot stock and the sherry and bring to the boil, stirring until the sauce is smooth.

3. Return the garlic and veal to the casserole, add the parsley and season with salt and pepper. Cover and simmer for about 1 hour until the veal is tender.

4. Remove the veal from the casserole and purée the sauce or rub it through a sieve. Return both veal and sauce to the casserole and add the olives. Reheat gently before serving.

Serves 4

Eggs

*Classic combinations of eggs
with onions, peppers and
other vegetables make
Spanish egg dishes so
distinctive.*

ish

Eggs with Courgettes

Ingredients

450 g/1 lb courgettes, thinly sliced
Salt
75 ml/5 tbsp olive oil
2 onions, sliced
6 eggs, beaten
Freshly ground black pepper
30 ml/2 tbsp chopped fresh parsley

Method

1. Place the courgettes in a colander and sprinkle with salt. Leave to stand for 15 minutes then rinse and drain well.

2. Heat the oil and fry the onions until just softened. Add the courgettes and fry for about 15 minutes until tender, turning carefully.

3. Season the beaten eggs with salt and pepper. Pour the eggs into the pan and cook until the eggs are just set and golden brown on the base and just lightly set on top. Serve sprinkled with parsley.

Serves 4

2 Spanish Omelette

Ingredients

> 60 ml/4 tbsp olive oil
> 900 g/2 lb potatoes, diced
> 2 onions, chopped
> 5 eggs, beaten
> 2.5 ml/½ tsp salt

Method

1. Heat the oil and fry the potatoes and onions over a low heat until tender but not browned, turning them gently.

2. Remove the potatoes from the pan with a slotted spoon and place them in a bowl. Add the eggs and salt and stir gently.

3. Reheat the oil, adding a little more if necessary. Pour the egg mixture into the pan and cook over a medium heat until the omelette is set and golden on the bottom, shaking the pan occasionally.

4. Hold a plate over the top of the pan and turn it upside down so that the omelette falls on to the plate. Slide it back into the pan and cook until the second side is golden brown. Serve at once cut into squares for tapas, or into wedges for lunch, supper or picnics.

Serves 4

3 Piperade

Ingredients

2 red peppers
75 ml/5 tbsp olive oil
5 cloves garlic, crushed
1 onion, chopped
75 g/3 oz ham, chopped
3 tomatoes, skinned and chopped
7 eggs, beaten
Salt and freshly ground black pepper

Method

1. Grill the peppers until the skins are lightly charred on all sides. Place them in a plastic bag, seal the tops and leave until cool enough to handle then strip off the skins, discard the stem and seeds and slice them into strips.

2. Heat all but 15 ml/1 tbsp of the oil and fry the garlic and onion until soft. Add the ham and stir together well then add the tomatoes and pepper and fry for about 20 minutes until the mixture is well blended. Remove from the pan.

3. Season the beaten eggs with salt and pepper. Heat the reserved oil then pour the eggs into the pan and stir over a low heat until just beginning to set. Add the pepper sauce and stir gently into the egg. Cover and cook for a further 4 minutes. Serve at once.

Serves 4

4 Scrambled Egg with Mushrooms

Ingredients

60 ml/4 tbsp olive oil
225 g/8 oz wild mushrooms or button mushrooms,
coarsely chopped
3 cloves garlic, crushed
8 eggs, beaten
Salt and freshly ground black pepper
30 ml/2 tbsp chopped fresh parsley

Method

1. Heat the oil and fry the mushrooms until tender and most of the liquid has evaporated. Add the garlic and fry for 3 minutes.

2. Season the beaten eggs with salt and pepper. Pour into the pan and stir the ingredients together gently over a low heat until the eggs are just set but still creamy. Serve sprinkled with parsley.

Serves 4

5 | Crispy-Fried Eggs

Ingredients

5 eggs
50 g/2 oz/½ cup plain flour
100 g/4 oz breadcrumbs
90 ml/6 tbsp olive oil

Method

1. Bring a large pan of water to the boil, break in the eggs and poach them for about 4 minutes until the white is firm. Remove from the pan with a slotted spoon and drain well.

2. Dust the eggs with the flour, shaking off any excess. Beat the remaining egg and dip the eggs in the egg then in the breadcrumbs.

3. Heat the oil and fry the poached eggs for a few minutes until crisp and golden.

Serves 4

6 Toasted Meringue Eggs

Ingredients

4 slices bread
50 g/2 oz butter
4 eggs, separated
100 g/4 oz Gruyère cheese, finely grated
Pinch of cayenne pepper
Pinch of salt

Method

1. Toast the bread on both sides then butter it and arrange it in a shallow ovenproof dish.

2. Place 1 egg yolk on each slice of bread. Whisk the egg whites until stiff then carefully fold in the cheese. Spoon the mixture over the toast slices and sprinkle with cayenne and salt to taste.

3. Bake in a preheated oven at 180°C/350°F/gas mark 4 for about 10 minutes until the egg is cooked.

Serves 4

7 | Eggs with Scallops

Ingredients

12 scallops
Juice of 1 lemon
6 eggs
30 ml/2 tbsp milk
Salt and freshly ground black pepper
30 ml/2 tbsp olive oil
8 raw, unpeeled prawns
15 ml/1 tbsp chopped fresh parsley

Method

1. Place the scallops in a preheated oven at 180°C/350°F/gas mark 4 for about 4 minutes until the shells open; discard any that remain closed. Remove the scallops from the shells and transfer to a dish. Sprinkle with the lemon juice and leave to stand for 20 minutes.

2. Pat the scallops dry on kitchen paper and chop them coarsely. Beat the eggs and milk and season with salt and pepper. Heat half the oil, pour in the eggs and scallops and stir gently over a low heat until just cooked but still creamy.

3. Meanwhile, heat the remaining oil and fry the prawns until they turn pink. Arrange the eggs on a warm serving plate, surround with the prawns and serve sprinkled with parsley.

Serves 4

Vegetables, Pulses and Rice

General Notes

Peppers, tomatoes and onions feature heavily in Spanish vegetable dishes but there are many other exciting and delicious recipes for a whole range of fresh vegetables, which the Spaniards enjoy in season.

Chick peas are a particular favourite and feature in many dishes, as do other delicious pulses.

Rice is a Moorish introduction which has been taken into the Spanish cooking, giving rise to the most widely-known dish in the repertoire: paella.

1 Asparagus with Poached Eggs

Ingredients

900 g/2 lb asparagus
Salt
4 eggs
15 ml/1 tsp white wine vinegar
30 ml/2 tbsp olive oil
15 ml/1 tbsp plain flour
Freshly ground black pepper
30 ml/2 tbsp chopped fresh parsley

Method

1. Cut off the hard bases of the asparagus and peel the stems, as necessary. Simmer the trimmings in a pan of boiling salted water for 15 minutes then strain and reserve the cooking liquid. Add the asparagus stems to the liquid and simmer gently for about 10 to 15 minutes until tender.

2. Meanwhile, poach the eggs in simmering water with the wine vinegar and keep them warm.

3. Heat the oil in a flameproof casserole, stir in the flour and cook for 1 minute. Remove from the heat and stir in 250 ml/8 fl oz/1 cup of the asparagus cooking water. Return to the heat and bring back to a simmer, stirring continuously. Season to taste with salt and pepper.

4. Add the asparagus and the eggs to the sauce and simmer until heated through. Serve sprinkled with parsley.

Serves 4

2 Catalan-Style Aubergines

Ingredients

2 aubergines, peeled and cubed
Salt
60 ml/4 tbsp olive oil
100 g/4 oz/1 cup hazelnuts
45 ml/3 tbsp stock or water
1 onion, chopped
4 cloves garlic, chopped
3 tomatoes, skinned and chopped
2.5 ml/½ tsp ground cinnamon
Freshly ground black pepper
3 sprigs fresh parsley

Method

1. Place the aubergines in a colander and sprinkle with salt. Leave to stand for 15 minutes then rinse in cold water, drain and pat dry.

2. Heat the oil and fry the hazelnuts until lightly browned. Remove from the pan with a slotted spoon and leave to cool slightly. Grind the hazelnuts in a mortar and pestle or in a food processor then mix them with the stock and put to one side.

3. Reheat the oil and fry the aubergine until lightly browned. Add the onion and garlic and fry for 2 minutes. Add the nuts, tomatoes and cinnamon and season to taste with salt and pepper. Simmer for about 15 minutes until the aubergines are very tender then serve garnished with parsley.

Serves 4

3 Broad Beans with Ham

Ingredients

120 ml/4 fl oz/½ cup olive oil
6 cloves garlic, chopped
450 g/1 lb shelled broad beans
100 g/4 oz Serrano ham or cured ham, diced
Salt and freshly ground black pepper
30 ml/2 tbsp chopped fresh mint

Method

1. Heat the oil and fry the garlic for 1 minute. Add the beans and stir until well coated in the garlic-flavoured oil. Add the ham, cover tightly and cook for about 20 minutes until the beans are tender, adding a little water during cooking if necessary.

2. Season with salt and pepper after cooking and serve sprinkled with mint.

Serves 4

Beans with Peppers

Ingredients

2 red peppers
75 ml/5 tbsp olive oil
450 g/1 lb green beans
4 cloves garlic, chopped
50 g/2 oz Serrano ham or cured ham, cut into slivers
15 ml/1 tbsp chopped fresh parsley
Salt and freshly ground black pepper

Method

1. Brush the peppers with a little of the oil and grill under a hot grill, turning frequently, until the skins are charred. Place them in a plastic bag until cool enough to handle then slide off the skins and discard the stems and seeds. Cut or tear the flesh into strips.

2. Meanwhile, blanch the beans in boiling water for about 4 minutes until almost tender and still very crisp. Drain well.

3. Heat the remaining oil and fry the garlic and ham until the garlic is lightly browned. Add the peppers, beans and parsley and season with salt and pepper. Simmer, stirring, for a few minutes until well combined and heated through. The beans should be just tender but still crisp.

Serves 4

5 Fried Cauliflower

Ingredients

350 g/12 oz cauliflower florets
15 ml/1 tbsp salt
15 ml/1 tbsp chopped fresh parsley
45 ml/3 tbsp white wine vinegar
45 ml/3 tbsp water
2 eggs, beaten
90 ml/6 tbsp olive oil

Method

1. Place the cauliflower florets in a large bowl. Mix together the salt, parsley, wine vinegar and water, pour over the cauliflower and stir well. Leave to marinate for 30 minutes, stirring occasionally.

2. Drain the cauliflower and pat it dry with kitchen paper. Dip it in the beaten eggs.

3. Heat the oil and fry the cauliflower for about 10 minutes until just tender but still crisp and lightly browned on all sides.

Serves 4

6 Chicory with Roquefort Cream

Ingredients

8 small heads chicory
Salt
15 ml/1 tbsp butter
250 ml/8 fl oz/1 cup single cream
75 g/3 oz Roquefort cheese, crumbled
Freshly ground black pepper

Method

1. Cook the chicory in boiling salted water for about 15 minutes until tender.

2. Melt the butter then stir in the cream and bring slowly to a simmer. Stir in the cheese and season to taste with salt and pepper.

3. Drain the chicory thoroughly, pressing out any excess water, then arrange on a warmed serving plate. Pour over the sauce and serve at once.

Serves 4

7 Stuffed Courgettes

Ingredients

4 medium courgettes
90 ml/6 tbsp olive oil
1 onion, chopped
3 ripe tomatoes, skinned and chopped
100 g/4 oz minced pork
100 g/4 oz minced beef
Salt and freshly ground black pepper
5 ml/1 tsp oregano
15 ml/1 tbsp plain flour
30 ml/2 tbsp breadcrumbs
30 ml/2 tbsp grated Gruyère cheese

Method

1. Halve the courgettes lengthways, scoop out the centre flesh with a spoon and chop the flesh.

2. Heat the oil and fry the onion and tomatoes for 10 minutes. Add the courgette flesh and fry for 4 minutes. Add the pork and beef, season with salt, pepper and oregano and simmer for 5 minutes, stirring frequently. Sprinkle with the flour then stir it into the mixture and remove from the heat.

3. Stuff the mixture into the courgette halves and place them in a shallow baking dish. Sprinkle with breadcrumbs and cheese and bake in a preheated oven at 180°C/350°F/gas mark 4 for 20 minutes until golden brown.

Serves 4

8 Mushrooms with Serrano Ham

Ingredients

450 g/1 lb mushrooms
90 ml/6 tbsp olive oil
4 cloves garlic, chopped
100 g/4 oz Serrano or cured ham, diced
15 ml/1 tbsp chopped fresh parsley
Salt and freshly ground black pepper

Method

1. Wash and dry the mushrooms thoroughly.

2. Heat the oil and fry the garlic until lightly browned. Add the ham and fry for 1 minute. Add the mushrooms and parsley and season with salt and pepper. Simmer over a low heat for about 30 minutes until most of the mushroom liquid has evaporated.

Serves 4

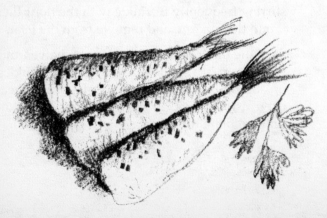

9 Escalivada

Ingredients

1 aubergine
2 red peppers
1 onion
2 tomatoes
30 ml/2 tbsp olive oil
30 ml/2 tbsp lemon juice
Salt and freshly ground black pepper

Method

1. Cut all the vegetables in half and brush the skins with half the olive oil. Place under a grill or in a hot oven and cook until the skins are charred. Leave until cool enough to handle then peel them and tear the flesh into strips.

2. Place the vegetables in a bowl. Mix the remaining oil with the lemon juice and season with salt and pepper. Pour over the vegetables and serve warm or cold with grilled meats.

Serves 4

10 Stuffed Peppers

Ingredients

8 red peppers
Flour for dusting
2 eggs, beaten
Oil for deep-frying

For the stuffing:
75 ml/5 tbsp olive oil
1 onion, chopped
2 cloves garlic, chopped
15 ml/1 tbsp chopped fresh parsley
100 g/4 oz Serrano or cured ham, chopped
175 g/6 oz minced beef
15 ml/1 tbsp plain flour
Salt and freshly ground black pepper

For the sauce:
90 ml/6 tbsp olive oil
1 red chilli pepper, chopped
1 onion, chopped
5 tomatoes, skinned and chopped
175 ml/6 fl oz/¾ cup dry white wine
175 ml/6 fl oz/¾ cup stock

Method

1. Grill the peppers, turning frequently, until the skin is charred then place in a plastic bag and leave until cool enough to handle. Carefully remove the stem and seeds and slide off the skin.

2. To make the stuffing, heat the oil and fry the onion, garlic and parsley for 10 minutes. Add the ham and beef and fry for 10 minutes until the meat is cooked. Add the flour, season with salt and pepper and cook over a low heat for 20 minutes. Leave to cool.

3. To make the sauce, heat the oil and fry the chilli pepper and onion for 5 minutes. Add the tomatoes, wine and stock, season with salt and pepper and simmer for 20 minutes. Rub through a sieve and set aside.

4. Fill the peppers with the stuffing and close the tops with cocktail sticks. Dust with flour then dip in the beaten eggs. Heat the oil until very hot then fry the peppers for about 15 minutes until lightly browned. Drain well and place in a shallow ovenproof dish. Pour over the sauce and cook in a preheated oven at 180°C/350°F/gas mark 4 for about 20 minutes.

Serves 4

11 Potatoes and Onions

Ingredients

150 ml/¼ pt/⅔ cup olive oil
450 g/l lb potatoes, thinly sliced
3 onions, sliced
1 red pepper, cut into strips
2 cloves garlic, chopped
2.5 ml/½ tsp ground cumin
2.5 ml/½ tsp paprika
90 ml/6 tbsp dry white wine
90 ml/6 tbsp water or stock
Salt and freshly ground black pepper
15 ml/1 tbsp chopped fresh parsley

Method

1. Heat half the oil in a large frying pan. Add the potatoes, onions, pepper and garlic in layers then pour on the remaining oil. Fry until the potatoes are beginning to brown, turning occasionally.

2. Mix together the cumin, paprika, wine and water or stock and season with salt and pepper. Pour over the potatoes, bring to the boil then cover and simmer for about 30 minutes until the potatoes are tender. Leave to stand for 5 minutes before serving sprinkled with parsley

Serves 4

12 | Catalan Spinach

Ingredients

25 g/1 oz raisins
900 g/2 lb spinach
Salt
90 ml/6 tbsp olive oil
100 g/4 oz Serrano or cured ham, chopped
25 g/1 oz/¼ cup pine nuts
Freshly ground black pepper

Method

1. Soak the raisins in warm water for 30 minutes then drain.

2. Meanwhile, clean the spinach well and remove the stems. Bring a saucepan of salted water to the boil, add the spinach and cook for 10 minutes. Drain well.

3. Heat the oil in a large frying pan and fry the ham for 2 minutes. Add the raisins and pine nuts then stir in the spinach and season with salt and pepper. Simmer gently for about 5 minutes then serve at once.

Serves 4

13 Lentils with Leeks and Mushrooms

Ingredients

450 g/1 lb green lentils
225 g/8 oz unsmoked boiling bacon
30 ml/2 tbsp olive oil
1 onion, chopped
2 leeks, sliced
225 g/8 oz mushrooms, sliced
3 tomatoes, skinned, seeded and chopped
2 sprigs fresh thyme
1 sprig fresh rosemary
Salt and freshly ground black pepper
45 ml/3 tbsp moscatel wine
Pinch of sugar

Method

1. Soak the lentils and bacon for at least 6 hours. Drain well.

2. Place the lentils and bacon in a pan and just cover with fresh water. Bring to the boil, skim, cover and simmer for 1 hour until tender.

3. Meanwhile, heat the oil and fry the onion for 5 minutes. Add the leeks and mushrooms and fry for a further 5 minutes. Add the tomatoes and herbs and simmer until soft.

4. Drain the lentils and bacon and shred the bacon. Add them to the pan and cook for 10 minutes. Season to taste with salt and pepper and stir in the wine and sugar.

Serves 6

14 Rice with Chicken

Ingredients

4 chicken portions
1.2 l/2 pts/5 cups chicken stock
30 ml/2 tbsp olive oil
1 onion, finely chopped
3 cloves garlic, crushed
225 g/8 oz medium-grain rice
Salt and freshly ground black pepper
30 ml/2 tbsp chopped fresh parsley

Method

1. Place the chicken and stock in a saucepan, bring to the boil and simmer for about 40 minutes until the chicken is cooked.

2. Heat the oil and fry the onion and garlic until soft but not browned. Stir in the rice until it is well coated in the oil.

3. Remove the chicken from the stock and keep it warm. Pour a little of the hot stock into the rice and stir until it is absorbed. Gradually add the remaining stock and simmer for about 20 minutes until the rice is tender. Season with salt and pepper.

4. Arrange the rice on a warmed serving plate, surround with the chicken and serve sprinkled with parsley.

Serves 4

15 Paella

Ingredients

8 clams or mussels, scrubbed
225 g/8 oz squid
75 ml/5 tbsp olive oil
4 cloves garlic
1 bay leaf
450 g/1 lb raw, unpeeled prawns
1 small chicken, cut into small pieces
225 g/8 oz lean pork, cubed
1 onion, chopped
1 green pepper, cut into strips
2 large tomatoes, skinned
Water or stock
Few strands of saffron
6 black peppercorns
2.5 ml/½ tsp paprika
450 g/1 lb medium-grain rice
50 g/2 oz frozen peas
200 g/7 oz canned red pimento, cut into strips

Method

1. Place the clams or mussels in a large pan with a little water, cover and place over a high heat for about 5 minutes until they open. Discard any that remain closed. Remove and discard the top shells, reserve the shellfish in the half shell and reserve the liquid.

2. Clean the squid and pull the body from the tentacles. Cut off the tentacles and discard the body and innards. Remove the outer membrane and the plastic-like quill. Cut the body into rings.

3. Heat half the oil and fry the garlic and bay leaf until lightly browned. Remove from the pan. Fry the prawns for a few minutes until they turn pink then remove them from the pan. Add the chicken and pork fry until lightly browned. Add the onion and pepper and fry for 2 minutes. Add the prepared squid and fry for 2 minutes. Add the remaining oil, raise the heat to high, and add the tomatoes, stirring well.

4. Make up the shellfish cooking liquid to 900 ml/ 1½ pts/3¾ cups with water or stock. Pour it into the pan and bring to the boil. Add the reserved garlic and bay leaf and season with the saffron, pepper and paprika. Simmer for about 5 minutes.

5. Stir in the rice and bring back to the boil then simmer, shaking the pan occasionally by not stirring, for 10 minutes. Add the peas and simmer until all the liquid has been absorbed and the rice is almost tender.

6. Arrange the reserved prawns, clams and mussels on top of the pan and garnish with the pimento. Cover and leave to stand for 15 minutes before serving from the paella pan.

7. If you use cooked, peeled prawns, add them at the end of cooking time so that they just heat through.

Serves 6 to 8

16 Rice with Prawns

Ingredients

45 ml/3 tbsp olive oil
2 onions, chopped
4 cloves garlic, chopped
225 g/8 oz tomatoes, skinned, seeded and quartered
225 g/8 oz medium-grain rice
450 ml/¾ pt/2 cups boiling water
5 ml/1 tsp paprika
Salt and freshly ground black pepper
225 g/8 oz cooked, peeled prawns

Method

1.   Heat the oil in a flameproof casserole and fry the
     onions and garlic until soft but not browned. Add
     the tomatoes and fry for a few minutes. Add the
     rice and stir the ingredients together well.

2.   Pour in the boiling water, add the paprika and
     season with salt and pepper. Bring to the boil,
     partially cover and simmer gently for about
     20 minutes until the rice is tender, adding a little
     more boiling water if necessary.

3.   Add the prawns and simmer until heated through.

Serves 4

Salads

*Salads are always served with
Spanish meals – with tapas, as
starters, or to accompany the
main dish. Often, a mixed salad
is arranged on a large platter in
the centre of the table, dressed
with olive oil and vinegar and
seasoned generously with salt
and pepper. The tasty dressing is
mopped up with crusty bread
once all the salad has been eaten.*

Artichoke and Pepper Salad

Ingredients

8 small tender globe artichokes
90 ml/6 tbsp olive oil
1 large red pepper, cut into strips
3 cloves garlic, chopped
3 ripe tomatoes, skinned and sliced
Salt and freshly ground black pepper
30 ml/2 tbsp white wine vinegar
12 black olives, stoned

Method

1. Cut off the stalks and tops of the buds from the artichokes and remove most of the outside leaves. Cook in boiling water for 20 minutes.

2. Heat 30 ml/2 tbsp of oil and fry the pepper for 4 minutes then add the garlic and continue to fry for 3 minutes. Add the tomatoes and simmer for 5 minutes. Season with salt and pepper.

3. Drain the artichokes. If they are very small they can be eaten whole. Otherwise, push out the hairy choke with a teaspoon and strip any hard leaf stubs from round the sides. Quarter them and add them to the pan.

4. Beat the wine vinegar with the remaining oil and season with salt and pepper. Turn the hot vegetables into a serving bowl and add the olives. Toss with the dressing and leave to cool before serving.

Serves 4

2 Carrot Salad

Ingredients

900 g/2 lb carrots, cut into matchsticks
Salt
60 ml/4 tbsp raisins
15 ml/1 tbsp pine nuts
1 onion, finely chopped
30 ml/2 tbsp chopped fresh parsley
3 cloves garlic, crushed
120 ml/4 fl oz/½ cup olive oil
60 ml/4 tbsp white wine vinegar
Juice of 1 lemon
Freshly ground black pepper
Few fresh mint leaves

Method

1. Place the carrots in a saucepan, just cover with cold water and add a pinch of salt. Bring to the boil, cover and simmer for about 5 minutes until the carrots are just tender but still crisp. Drain well then rinse in cold water.

2. Place the carrots in a bowl and mix with the raisins, pine nuts, onion and parsley.

3. Beat together the garlic, olive oil, wine vinegar and lemon juice and season with salt and pepper. Pour over the carrot mixture and toss together well. Leave to marinate in a cool place for 2 hours before serving garnished with a few mint leaves.

Serves 4

3 Lettuce and Anchovy Salad

Ingredients

4 little gem lettuces
90 ml/6 tbsp olive oil
30 ml/2 tbsp white wine vinegar
1 clove garlic, crushed
Salt and freshly ground black pepper
50 g/2 oz canned anchovy fillets, drained

Method

1. Chill the lettuce thoroughly.

2. Whisk together the olive oil, wine vinegar and garlic until emulsified and season with salt and pepper.

3. Cut the lettuces into 4 wedges and arrange on individual serving plates. Spoon over the dressing and arrange the anchovy fillets on top.

Serves 4

ESPAÑA

4 | Pepper Salad

Ingredients

6 red peppers
4 tomatoes, skinned, seeded and quartered
2 onions, chopped
90 ml/6 tbsp olive oil
30 ml/2 tbsp white wine vinegar
5 ml/1 tsp mild mustard
Salt and freshly ground black pepper
30 ml/2 tbsp chopped fresh parsley

Method

1. Grill the peppers under a hot grill, turning frequently, until the skin is charred. Place them in a plastic bag until cool enough to handle. Strip off the skin and discard the stem and seeds. Slice the flesh into strips.

2. Mix the pepper strips, tomatoes and onions in a serving bowl. Whisk together the oil, wine vinegar and mustard and season with salt and pepper. Stir in the parsley then pour the vinaigrette over the salad and toss gently.

Serves 4

5 Tomato Salad

Ingredients

4 hard tomatoes, sliced
300 g/11 oz ripe tomatoes, skinned and seeded
4 cloves garlic, finely chopped
2.5 ml/½ tsp salt
200 ml/7 fl oz/scant 1 cup olive oil
15 ml/1 tbsp sherry vinegar
Freshly ground black pepper
2.5 ml/½ tsp ground cumin

Method

1. Arrange the salad tomatoes in a serving bowl.

2. Purée the ripe tomatoes with the garlic and salt then slowly add the oil and vinegar to make a smooth emulsion. Season to taste with salt and pepper. Pour over the tomatoes and sprinkle with cumin.

Serves 4

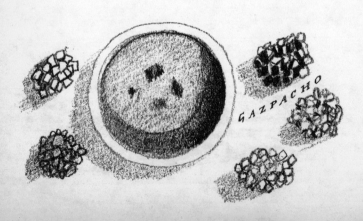

GAZPACHO

Desserts

Fresh fruit is the most common dessert in Spain, and it provides the perfect ending to any meal. Experiment with the new exotic fruits now available to create your own fresh fruit salads.

1 Apples with Wine

Ingredients

4 large dessert apples
50 g/2 oz almonds, chopped
90 ml/6 tbsp honey
2.5 ml/½ tsp ground cinnamon
30 ml/2 tbsp butter
300 ml/½ pt/1¼ cups dry white wine

Method

1. Core the apples and cut a line around the centre. Place them in a baking dish and fill the centres with nuts. Spoon the honey over the top, sprinkle with cinnamon and dot with butter.

2. Pour the wine around the apples and bake in a preheated oven at 200°C/400°F/gas mark 6 for about 30 minutes until soft. Serve hot or cold.

Serves 4

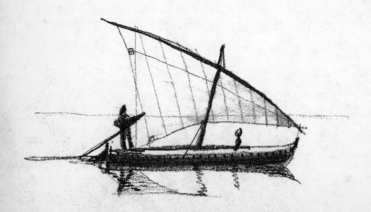

2 | Custard Tart

Ingredients

300 ml/½ pt/1¼ cups milk
1 strip lemon rind
1 cinnamon stick
450 g/1 lb Ricotta or cottage cheese
225 g/8 oz/1 cup caster sugar
4 eggs
100 g/4 oz biscuit crumbs
Freshly grated nutmeg

Method

1. Place the milk, lemon rind and cinnamon in a pan and bring to the boil. Remove from the heat.

2. Beat the cheese until smooth, sieving it beforehand if necessary. Beat in the sugar then gradually beat in the eggs. Discard the lemon rind and cinnamon then mix the milk and biscuit crumbs into the cheese.

3. Pour the mixture into a shallow baking dish and bake in a preheated oven at 180°C/350°F/gas mark 4 for about 45 minutes until set. Serve sprinkled with nutmeg.

Serves 4

3 Caramel Custard

Ingredients

> 200 g/7 oz/scant 1 cup caster sugar
> 45 ml/3 tbsp water
> 750 ml/1¼ pts/3 cups milk
> 1 cinnamon stick
> 1 piece lemon rind
> 3 eggs
> 2 egg yolks

Method

1. Dissolve 100 g/4 oz/½ cup of sugar in the water over a low heat and boil without stirring until the sugar turns golden. Remove from the heat and pour into 6 individual ramekin dishes. Stand them in a baking tin filled with water to come half way up the sides of the dishes.

2. Bring the milk to the boil with the cinnamon and lemon rind then remove from the heat.

3. Beat the eggs and egg yolks with the remaining sugar. Remove the cinnamon and lemon rind from the milk, pour it into the eggs and beat well. Pour the custard through a sieve into the ramekins and bake in a preheated oven at 180°C/350°F/gas mark 4 for about 45 minutes until the custards are set.

4. Leave the custards to cool then chill until ready to serve. Unmould on to individual plates.

Serves 6

4 Sugared Wine Toasts

Ingredients

8 thick slices stale French bread
120 ml/4 fl oz/½ cup red wine
2 eggs, beaten
60 ml/4 tbsp olive oil
Sugar for sprinkling
Pinch of ground cinnamon

Method

1. Dip the bread slices on both sides into the wine then into the beaten egg.

2. Heat the oil and fry the coated bread for a few minutes until crisp and golden. Drain on a platter coated with sugar while you cook the remaining slices then transfer to a serving plate and serve dusted with sugar and cinnamon.

Serves 4

5 Chocolate Turnovers

Ingredients

90 ml/6 tbsp olive oil
90 ml/6 tbsp dry white wine
Pinch of salt
Pinch of bicarbonate of soda
350 g/12 oz/3 cups plain flour

For the filling:
450 ml/¾ pt/2 cups milk
60 ml/4 tbsp cocoa powder
60 ml/4 tbsp granulated sugar
30 ml/2 tbsp cornflour

Oil for frying
Sugar for dusting

Method

1. Mix together the oil, wine, salt, bicarbonate of soda in a bowl. Place the flour in a bowl and make a well in the centre. Gradually add the oil mixture and work into the flour. Knead the dough lightly into a ball.

2. In a saucepan, mix 300 ml/½ pt/1¼ cups of milk with the cocoa powder over a low heat. Add the sugar and bring to the boil. Mix the remaining milk with the cornflour then stir it into the pan and simmer, stirring, until the mixture thickens. Remove from the heat and leave to cool.

3. Roll out the dough on a lightly floured surface and cut into 10 cm/4 in rounds. Brush the chocolate cream over the surface of the rounds then fold them in half and press the edges together firmly.

4. Heat 2.5 cm/1 in of oil in a frying pan. Add the turnovers a few at a time and fry for about 5 minutes until lightly browned, turning once. Remove from the pan, drain well then toss in sugar before serving.

Serves 4

6 Fried Milk

Ingredients

> 600 ml/1 pt/2½ cups milk
> ½ cinnamon stick
> 1 piece lemon rind
> 150 g/4 oz/¼ cup butter
> 250 g/9 oz/2½ cups plain flour
> 100 g/4 oz/½ cup caster sugar
> 4 eggs, separated
> 100 g/4 oz fine breadcrumbs
> Oil for frying
> Sugar for dusting

Method

1. Bring the milk to the boil with the cinnamon and lemon rind then leave to stand until required.

2. Melt the butter then stir in 175 g/6 oz/1½ cups of flour and cook over a low heat, stirring, for 1 minute. Stir in the sugar. Strain the hot milk into the pan, stirring constantly over a low heat until the custard thickens.

3. Remove from the heat and gradually beat in the egg yolks. Pour the mixture into a lightly oiled rectangular tin so that it is about 2 cm/¾ in deep. Leave to cool then chill for at least 2 hours.

4. Cut the batter into 5 cm/2 in squares. Dip in the remaining flour. Lightly beat the egg whites and dip the squares in the egg white then into the breadcrumbs.

5.   Heat the oil and fry the squares a few at a time for a few minutes until golden on both sides. Serve hot or cold sprinkled with sugar.

Serves 4

7 | Walnut Cream

Ingredients

100 g/4 oz/1 cup shelled walnuts
500 ml/17 fl oz/2¼ cups milk
100 g/4 oz/½ cup sugar
Strip of lemon rind
½ cinnamon stick
1 slice stale bread, crusts removed
100 ml/3½ fl oz/6½ tbsp single cream
Pinch of ground cinnamon

Method

1. Grind the nuts to a powder without allowing them to become oily.

2. Bring the milk to the boil with the sugar, lemon rind and cinnamon. Stir in the nuts and simmer for 30 minutes.

3. Crumble the bread, add it to the milk and simmer for 3 minutes. Remove the lemon rind and cinnamon.

4. Beat the mixture until creamy then stir in the cream. Pour into individual bowls and leave to cool. Chill in the refrigerator then dust lightly with cinnamon and serve very cold.

Serves 4

Cakes
and
Biscuits

*Spaniards often prefer to buy
their cakes and pastries rather
than make them at home, but
there are some lovely, simple
recipes you can try.*

1 Almond Biscuits

Ingredients

> 100 g/4 oz plain biscuits
> 225 g/8 oz almonds
> 300 ml/½ pt/1¼ cups water
> 225 g/8 oz/1 cup caster sugar
> 10 ml/2 tsp grated lemon rind
> 6 eggs
> 2 egg yolks
> 15 ml/1 tbsp icing sugar
> Freshly grated nutmeg

Method

1. Arrange the biscuits in the base of a greased square tin.

2. Toast the almonds in a dry pan until golden then grind them.

3. Place the water, sugar and lemon rind in a pan, bring to the boil and simmer until thick. Stir in the ground almonds.

4. Beat the eggs and egg yolks then stir them into the almond mixture and spread the mixture over the biscuits. Bake in a preheated oven at 180°C/350°F/gas mark 4 for 35 minutes. Leave to cool in the tin then sprinkle with icing sugar and nutmeg and serve cut into squares.

Serves 4

2 Turron

Ingredients

450 g/1 lb ground almonds
450 g/1 lb/2 cups caster sugar
6 egg yolks, beaten
1 egg white, beaten

Method

1. Mix together the almonds and sugar then gradually stir in the egg yolks and beat well. Stir in the egg whites.

2. Line a shallow cake tin with greased greaseproof paper and spoon the mixture into the tin. Cover with more greased paper, place a weight on top and leave to set for 48 hours before cutting into squares.

Serves 4

3 Magdalenas

Ingredients

225 g/8 oz/1 cup caster sugar
75 ml/5 tbsp olive oil
3 eggs
6 egg whites
450 g/1 lb/4 cups plain flour

Method

1.   Beat the sugar and oil together then beat in the
      eggs. Whisk the egg whites until stiff then beat
      them into the mixture. Gradually beat in the flour
      until the mixture is of a dropping consistency.

2.   Spoon the mixture into greased cake tins and bake
      in a preheated oven at 200°C/400°F/gas mark 6 for
      about 12 minutes until lightly golden.

Serves 4

4 Churros

Ingredients

300 ml/½ pt/1¼ cups water
45 ml/3 tbsp olive oil
2.5 ml/½ tsp salt
200 g/7 oz/1¾ cups plain flour
Oil for deep-frying
50 g/2 oz/¼ cup caster sugar

Method

1. Put the water, oil and salt in a heavy-based pan and bring to the boil. Add the flour and beat until the mixture is stiff and comes away from the sides of the pan. Remove from the heat.

2. Heat the oil and fry spoonfuls of the dough, a few at a time, until golden brown. Remove and drain on kitchen paper then sprinkle with sugar and serve with hot chocolate.

Serves 4

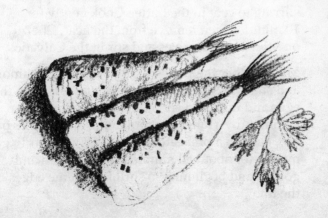

5　Apple Cake

Ingredients

175 g/6 oz/¾ cup butter
150 g/5 oz/1¼ cups plain flour
6 Cox's apples, peeled cored and sliced
30 ml/2 tbsp Calvados
10 ml/2 tsp baking powder
5 ml/1 tsp ground cinnamon
175 g/6 oz/¾ cup caster sugar
3 eggs
45 ml/3 tbsp milk

For the glaze:
60 ml/4 tbsp apricot jam
15 ml/1 tbsp Calvados
5 ml/1 tsp cornflour
10 ml/2 tsp water

Method

1. Use a little butter to grease a spring-form cake tin. Melt the remaining butter and add the apples, stirring to coat in the butter. Cook gently for 10 minutes then remove from the heat. Chop one-third of the apples and stir in the Calvados.

2. Mix together the flour, baking powder, cinnamon and sugar then add the apple mixture. Beat in the eggs and milk and spoon the mixture into the baking tin. Arrange the remaining apple slices on top. Bake in a preheated oven at 180°C/350°F/gas mark 4 for about 50 minutes or until risen and golden and beginning to shrink from the edges of the tin.

3. Warm the jam and Calvados. Blend the cornflour and water to a paste then stir it into the warm mixture. Simmer for about 3 minutes until clear then brush the top of the cake with the glaze. Leave to cool for 30 minutes then remove the sides of the tin. Rewarm the remaining glaze and brush again over the cake. Serve warm or cold.

Makes 1 x 23 cm/9 in cake

6 Basque Gâteau

Ingredients

200 g/7 oz butter, softened
200 g/7 oz/scant 1 cup caster sugar
2 egg yolks
300 g/10 oz/2½ cups plain flour
10 ml/2 tsp baking powder
Finely grated rind of 1 lemon
Pinch of salt
50 g/2 oz/⅓ cup raisins
30 ml/2 tbsp brandy

For the custard:
250 ml/8 fl oz/1 cup milk
1 cinnamon stick
1 vanilla pod
30 ml/2 tbsp brandy
2 egg yolks
30 ml/2 tbsp caster sugar
15 ml/1 tbsp plain flour
Pinch of salt
15 ml/1 tbsp butter

Method

1.   Cream the butter and sugar until light then beat in
        the egg yolks. Gradually add the flour, baking
        powder, lemon rind and salt and mix to a firm
        dough. Cover and refrigerate for 1 hour.

2.   Meanwhile, soak the raisins in the brandy.

3.   To make the custard, place the milk, cinnamon
        stick and vanilla pod in a saucepan and bring to
        the boil. Remove from the heat and stir in the
        brandy.

4. Whisk the egg yolks, sugar, flour and salt in a bowl until smooth then place the bowl over a pan of gently simmering water. Discard the vanilla and cinnamon then pour the hot milk into the egg mixture. Stir over a gentle heat for about 10 minutes until the sauce thickens. Remove from the heat and stir in the butter. Leave to cool.

5. Roll out half the cake dough and use it to line a greased and floured 20 cm/8 in flan tin. Spread with the custard then top with the remaining dough. Bake in a preheated oven at 200°C/400°F/gas mark 6 for about 35 minutes until golden brown. Leave to cool before turning out of the tin.

Makes 1 x 20 cm/8 in cake

Tortilla

7 Marsala Cake

Ingredients

8 eggs
350 g/12 oz/1½ cups granulated sugar
350 g/12 oz/3 cups plain flour
10 ml/2 tsp butter

For the syrup:
300 ml/½ pt/1¼ cups water
350 g/12 oz/1½ cups brown sugar
350 g/12 oz/1½ cups granulated sugar
400 ml/14 fl oz/1¾ cups Marsala wine
15 ml/1 tbsp ground cinnamon

Method

1. Heat an earthenware bowl in the oven for several minutes until hot. Add the eggs and sugar and beat to a thick syrup. Add 275 g/10 oz/ 2½ cups of flour a little at a time and beat until the ingredients are well mixed.

2. Grease a shallow metal cake tin with the butter and sprinkle with the remaining flour. Pour the cake batter into the pan and bake in a preheated oven at 190°C/375°F/gas mark 5 for 45 minutes.

3. Meanwhile, heat the water and sugars and simmer over a medium heat for about 20 minutes until a thick syrup forms. Remove from the heat and leave to cool. Stir in the wine.

4. Remove the cake from the oven and leave to cool slightly before turning out of the tin. Cut into slices and arrange on a serving plate. Pour over the syrup and sprinkle with cinnamon before serving.

Makes 1 x 23 cm/9 in cake

8 Spanish Doughnuts

Ingredients

350 g/12 oz/½ cups caster sugar
150 ml/¼ pt/⅔ cup olive oil
150 ml/¼ pt/⅔ cup orange juice
Grated rind of ½ lemon
5 ml/1 tsp ground cinnamon
2.5 ml/½ tsp ground anise
750 g/1¾ lb/7 cups plain flour
2 eggs, separated
10 ml/2 tsp bicarbonate of soda
Oil for deep-frying

Method

1. Mix together 100 g/4 oz of sugar, the oil, orange juice, lemon rind, cinnamon and anise. Add half the flour then add the egg yolks and bicarbonate of soda.

2. Beat the egg whites until stiff, then fold them into the mixture. Gradually work in the remaining flour until the dough is firm and no longer sticky.

3. Roll the dough into a long sausage shape and cut off pieces of the dough. Shape into rings.

4. Heat the oil and deep-fry the doughnuts a few at a time until puffed up and golden brown. Remove and drain then sprinkle with the remaining sugar and serve hot or cold.

Serves 4

Drinks

1 Sherry

The centre of sherry production is Jerez de la Frontera in southern Spain, and true sherry can be made nowhere else. Now that we have a range of quality sherries readily available, more people outside Spain are beginning to understand what a delicate and sophisticated drink it is.

Sherries are produced by a complicated and subtle process. Dry wines are casked with a gap left at the top of the cask so that a layer of yeast, a 'flor' grows on the surface. By a system known as 'solera', wines ready to be bottled are blended with younger wines and then fortified. Some wines do not develop a flor and they are fortified and sometimes sweetened for the export market, although in Spain, most sherry is dry.

These are the main types of sherry:

Manzanilla sherries are dry and delicate.

Finos are the finest dry white sherries. They are sometimes sweetened to make pale cream.

Amontillado are fino sherries which were not considered good enough and have been left to mature further to make a darker sherry which is usually sweetened for export.

Palo cortado lies between an amontillado and an oloroso.

Oloroso sherries are those which have not developed a flor. They are sweetened for the export market.

2 Sangria

Ingredients

> 120 ml/4 fl oz/½ cup brandy or Cointreau
> 100 g/4 oz/½ cup sugar
> Sliced fresh fruit such as oranges, bananas, apples and
>   strawberries
> 1 bottle red wine, chilled
> Soda water

Method

1. Stir the brandy or Cointreau and sugar together until the sugar has dissolved. Add the fruit, stir well then refrigerate until required.

2. Stir in the wine and dilute to taste with soda water.

Serves 6

3 Iced Lemonade

Ingredients

10 lemons
1 l/1¾ pts/4¼ cups boiling water
350 g/12 oz/1½ cups sugar
Crushed ice

Method

1. Thinly pare strips of zest from the lemons and squeeze the juice. Place the zest in a bowl, pour over the boiling water and leave to cool.

2. Remove the lemon zest and stir in the sugar and lemon juice. Refrigerate until required.

3. When ready to serve, dilute the lemonade with an equal quantity of water and serve in a glass half-filled with crushed ice.

Makes 20 glasses

ESPAÑA

4 Hot Chocolate

Ingredients

100 g/4 oz plain chocolate, grated
900 ml/1½ pts/3¾ cups milk
15 ml/1 tbsp cornflour
60 ml/4 tbsp sugar

Method

1. Place the chocolate and half the milk in a saucepan over a low heat and stir until the chocolate has dissolved.

2. Whisk the cornflour and sugar into the remaining milk then stir it into the pan and simmer for about 5 minutes, whisking continuously, until the chocolate is smooth and thick.

Serves 4

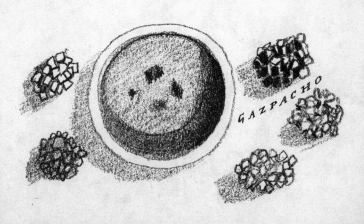

Sauces

Many of the sauces used in Spanish cooking are an integral part of the process of cooking the dish. However, these sauces will give you a flavour of some of the basic sauces used in Spanish cuisine.

1 | Almond Sauce

Ingredients

2 hard-boiled egg yolks
6 almonds, toasted
5 ml/1 tsp chopped fresh parsley
Salt and freshly ground black pepper
600 ml/1 pt/2½ cups milk

Method

1. Pound together the egg yolks, almonds and parsley and season with salt and pepper.

2. Stir in the milk and simmer gently over a low heat, stirring frequently, until reduced by half. Rub through and sieve and serve with grilled meats or fish.

Serves 4

2 Alioli Sauce

Ingredients

1 egg
4 cloves garlic
175 ml/6 fl oz/¾ cup olive oil
30 ml/2 tbsp white wine vinegar
2.5 ml/½ tsp salt

Method

1. Place the egg and garlic in a blender and process until smooth.

2. With the motor running, add the oil in a slow, steady stream until the sauce is thick and emulsified.

3. Add the wine vinegar and salt.

Serves 4

3 Potato Sauce

Ingredients

30 ml/2 tbsp olive oil
225 g/8 oz potatoes, chopped
2 tomatoes, skinned, seeded and chopped
1 red pepper, chopped
3 cloves garlic, chopped
1 bay leaf, crumbled
1 clove
600 ml/1 pt/2½ cups water, boiling
Salt and freshly ground black pepper

Method

1. Heat the oil and fry all the vegetables and herbs over a low heat for about 15 minutes until soft. Add the water, bring to the boil, and simmer for about 5 minutes, stirring continuously.

2. Rub the sauce through a sieve then return to the pan to reheat before serving with fish.

Serves 4

4 Romesco Sauce

Ingredients

50 g/2 oz dried red peppers
300 ml/½ pt/1¼ cups olive oil
100 g/4 oz/1 cup almonds
3 cloves garlic
1 slice white bread
Cayenne pepper
2.5 ml/½ tsp salt
Freshly ground black pepper
30 ml/2 tbsp brandy
30 ml/2 tbsp white wine vinegar
15 ml/1 tbsp tomato purée

Method

1. Cover the peppers with water in a saucepan, bring to the boil then simmer for 5 minutes. Remove from the heat and leave to soak for 20 minutes.

2. Heat 60 ml/4 tbsp of oil in a heavy-based pan and fry the almonds and garlic until lightly golden. Remove from the pan and put aside.

3. Reheat the oil and fry the bread until crisp. Remove from the oil and leave the oil to cool.

4. Split open the peppers and discard the stem and seeds. Scrape the flesh from the skin and place in a food processor with the nuts, garlic, bread, cayenne pepper, salt and pepper. Process until smooth.

5.   Add the brandy, wine vinegar and tomato purée then gradually add the remaining olive oil.

6.   Serve the sauce at room temperature with grilled dishes or add it to a sautéed dish at the end of the cooking time.

Serves 4

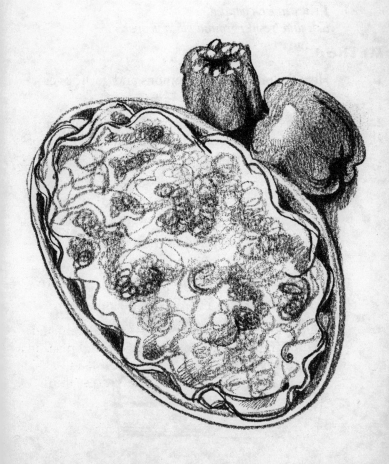

5 Tomato Sauce

Ingredients

120 ml/4 fl oz/½ cup olive oil
2 onions, chopped
1 clove garlic, chopped
450 g/1 lb tomatoes, skinned, seeded and chopped
1 red pepper, chopped
Salt and freshly ground black pepper

Method

1. Heat the oil and fry the onions and garlic over a low heat until soft.

2. Add the tomatoes and pepper and simmer for about 25 minutes until the sauce thickens. Season with salt and pepper.

Serves 4

6 | Walnut Sauce

Ingredients

100 g/4 oz/1 cup shelled walnuts
600 ml/1 pt/2½ cups milk

Method

1. Place the nuts in a bowl and pour over boiling water. When cool enough to handle, rub off the skins. Grind the nuts in a processor or mortar.

2. Mix the ground nuts with the milk and simmer over a low heat, stirring frequently, until reduced by half. Serve with pork.

Serves 4

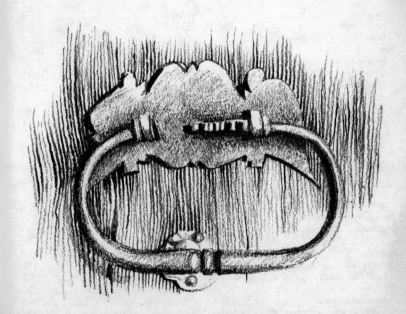

Index